D1707477

# CURIOUS?

**Start The Conversation**

J. E. Lukach

This book is dedicated to all the victims of this massive deception – those who died too soon, too suddenly, too senselessly, whether young or old, not because they sought to do harm, but because they strived to do good – for themselves, for their families and their friends, and even for those they did not know – all to serve an evil purpose. And to all who loved them and mourn their loss. May that loss enlighten others to the truth behind the lies, and save them from a similar fate.

*You never know how much you really believe anything until its truth or falsehood becomes a matter of life and death to you.*

C.S. Lewis

# Table of Contents

# Covid-19 Vaccines and Induced Anaphylaxis

Influenza A and B, commonly known as the flu, tend to show up predictably each year at the same time and is caused by a relatively benign corona virus. It is less of an illness and more a type of evidence that your body's immune system is doing what it is designed to do. Minor cold and flu symptoms are the way the body naturally detoxes, and it is only because such efforts are under appreciated that we have the arrogance to complain and ascribe the experience as illness.

The "pandemic" we are experiencing is little more than an average flu season that has been weaponized into something we are being told is far worse and quite unique – and it is, but only in rather insignificant ways. All the world's a stage as the saying goes. Welcome to the 'Covid Show.' The pandemic is nothing more than an average flu season, and as flu seasons go it is actually a fair amount below average in terms of annual recorded instances. It also ended last April.

Over the past two decades, a lot of unethical research has been going on which is known as gain-of-function research. This type of work seeks to run experiments that increase the capability, virulence and transmissibility of various pathogens. With the possible exception of creating bio-weapons, this type of activity has no useful purpose. It was for this reason that it was banned in the U.S. and elsewhere but, unfortunately, those wishing to continue the work managed to get around these restrictions, disguising it in various ways before simply moving the labs offshore and continuing to pursue their goals wherever they found a safe haven in which to do so.

Without getting into all the details of this activity, the stage hands of the Covid Show, the advancement of this research, and what it supposedly produced, can all be found in China, specifically the Wuhan Lab, at least that is what we have been told. For the purpose of this material, how this happened and the specifics of it, is of little import. I am going to deal rather directly with what came as a result of this work, but certain facts need to be understood, so I will briefly cover those to provide context.

## SARS-CoV2 and COVID-19

The terms SARS-CoV2 and COVID-19 are frequently and incorrectly used interchangeably. If we are to deal here in facts, we must take the greatest possible care to be precise in our use of such terms. COVID-19 does not refer to any particular disease with its own symtomology. It is more of an umbrella that covers far too broad a range of illnesses and symptoms than it is possible for one disease to have, and the net result of this ambiguity is confusion. SARS-CoV2, however, is quite specific and currently defined as a corona family pathogen, a virus whose actual existence is highly questionable, since there is not one solitary properly done isolation of it anywhere you would expect to find it, which includes the corpses of people said to have died as a result of catching it. And that one fact cannot be disputed or proven false, not by you or anyone else. Many have tried, and made worthy efforts to track this bug down, all without success. If anyone does have it isolated, they won't show you because that would allow someone to analyze it and discover everything it is not.

Truthfully, its existence is irrelevant, because a specially designed corona strain is not really required to pull off a pandemic scare. Any average flu bug will do, but let's assume

12

SARS-CoV2 is a thing and not get hung up on that. If it exists, it is a corona mutation that has been artificially bio-engineered through gain-of-function research to make it even more transmissible than it already is. Even with heightened transmissibility, it was never any more dangerous than any corona before it, since the symptoms caused by this infection are only life-threatening in cases where the immune system of person who contracts it is, for a variety of reasons, too weak to fight it off. And because this was a new strain, it had not made its way around the world yet, as all new mutations of corona bugs do. It was chosen to be the infamous "COVID-19," as will every future variant of it, because of its wide range of common symptoms and its ability to mutate.

It is this natural shape-shifting ability that has made it impossible in the past to defend against it with any sort of preventative vaccine product. Every such attempt has failed because every time an attempt was made, the resulting vaccine adversely affected the immune system it was supposed to empower. The biology here is complex but, simply put, the result of all previous attempts to create a vaccine for flu is that all the animal test subjects consistently died after being vaccinated.

## CV-19 Vaccines Provide Zero Immunity

Shockingly, the CV-19 vaccines being offered today are no different, and we would have known that had any animal testing been done. **That is why there wasn't any.** Despite this inherent danger, such vaccines are currently being administered as fast as possible to people all over the world, who are now scared to death in most cases, of a relatively benign pathogen that has been over-hyped as something it is not. And it is out of the sheer panic this mass media and governmental fear campaign has produced that many have been misled in an overly heavy-handed way. They have been allowed, even encouraged, to assume that a new kind of medical technology has overcome the problems of the past, and that these new mRNA vaccines provide immunity to SARS-CoV2.

The fact is, they don't, and nowhere in any of the testing data or product literature is immunity specifically stated as a benefit. In its place you will see a slippery statement like "Based on the evidence, we have reason to believe this product is safe and 95 percent effective in the prevention of SARS-CoV2."

*This is not the same as immunity.* It is telling you that the manufacturer believes its theoretical statement. They are not telling you a fact, and their claims of safety and efficacy are shameless statistical trickery. Not only is the pathogen not dangerous (any illness with a 99.97 percent survival rate is not dangerous), these vaccines provide nothing of value that cannot be obtained from simply eating healthy and taking a few vitamins, but what's worse, they are anything but benign. Any person seriously considering taking one of these vaccines, needs to understand what they actually are. All mRNA vaccine products are covert depopulation bio-weapons, designed specifically to cull the herd of undesirable humans, and I am going to not only prove this, but I am going to blow the lid off this plot using evidence taken from official medical reports and statements made by actual vaccine recipients who have fallen victim to the effects of these poison shots.

Because I smelled a rat very early on and could not believe how fast all my freedoms were being taken away, I became really angry with the whole Covid-imposed environment – the mandates, the mask orders, the curfews, the outrageous harassment I was subjected to by frightened hypochondriacs and mask police. I was personally assaulted, on a daily basis, from every direction. I watched the world just roll over and buy this scam. I could see this was rapidly getting far out of hand. It was shocking. There was no way this could be real, there would be bodies in the streets, and I saw nothing of the sort. I didn't know how I was going to do it at the time, but something had to be done, and it was then that I decided I had to take action.

To that end, I have been hard at work since this pandemic began, and I have put in thousands of hours of intense study of everything connected to it. What I am about to tell you in this book is the result of a tireless and obsessive effort, but the work is far from complete. I plan to release a lot more information in the future, but right now the most important aspect of this work is to expose what this vaccine is doing, or there won't be anyone left to properly maintain the society I miss. I can do that with near perfect clarity now, so pay attention. Your life depends on it. **If you get this vaccine you will die prematurely. It may take as long as a year or so, but trust me when I tell you, its only purpose is to kill you through the perversion of your own immune system, and it accomplishes this task extremely well. In that respect, it will actually turn out to be more than 95 percent effective.**

Everyone has a theory, and I have read them all. Many are very good and well-researched, and I have the highest respect for the people putting forth those ideas because they know way more than I do. They are on the right track. However, the problem I see is a common one: In my opinion, they cannot see the forest through the trees. On February 20th, 2021, I had a breakthrough in my work. I made a discovery that explained every adverse reaction report I had read about, and I have read tens of thousands of them.

I want to introduce you to a man who died more than a hundred years ago, but whose work is the cornerstone of the most diabolical eugenics effort ever devised – an effort that dwarfs Adolph Hitler's contribution to history. That man is Charles Richet.

# The Work of Charles Robert Richet

Charles R. Richet

Professor Charles Robert Richet was a French physiologist at the *Collège de France* known for his pioneering work in immunology. **In 1913, he won the Nobel Prize in Physiology or Medicine "in recognition of his work on anaphylaxis."[i]**

He was also an outspoken eugenicist with a hatred of Blacks. Richet was a proponent of eugenics, advocating sterilization and marriage prohibition for those with mental disabilities.

Richet expressed his eugenicist ideas in his 1919 book *La Sélection Humaine*. From 1920 to 1926, he presided over the French Eugenics Society. Psychologist Gustav Jahoda noted that Richet *"was a firm believer in the inferiority of Blacks, comparing black people to apes, and intellectually to imbeciles."*

## COVID-19 and the False Campaign of Fear

*Nearly everything the mass media repeats with regard to COVID-19 is false.*

This is an important historical footnote, because the CV-19 vaccines are a response to COVID-19, a mythical terror which is simply the common seasonal flu, covertly re-branded by the eugenist profiteers who currently infest organizations like the World Health Organization (WHO) and the Centers for Disease Control (CDC), as a serious 'novel' health threat, created in a bio-weapons lab, that was 'accidentally' released.

This frightening horror story allowed them to manufacture a global fear campaign that has only one goal: To make you so afraid of contracting a cold that you will line up for a vaccine to protect against it. The CV-19 vaccines are genetically engineered monstrosities, with a carefully designed flaw that can be hidden almost entirely and passed off as any number of adverse events that are as common with vaccine procedures as they are with flus, and this was the first clue. **Both of these symptom lists are virtually identical!**

The eugenics movement is alive and well, disguised as caring physicians, medical associations, research laboratories and philanthropic health organizations, and if you understand this, you can plainly see the influence and effect of this insidious eugenics movement in public policy everywhere now. Nearly everything the mass media repeats with regard to COVID-19 is false.

# The Discovery of Anaphylaxis

Back in 1913, Charles Richet made a very important contribution to the current generation of eugenicists with his Nobel Prize winning discovery of what he called "Anaphylaxis." Beyond this significant achievement, Richet did little else worthy of note. He was a "one-hit wonder" so to speak, after which he disappeared into history studying areas of parapsychology until his death in 1935. But in his 1913 Nobel acceptance speech[1], he outlined the results of his research into allergic reactions and even coined the term "Anaphylaxis." I strongly encourage everyone to read it.

This one speech provides all the answers needed to clearly explain everything being missed by doctors today, all of whom are completely baffled by the sheer scope of symtomology being attributed to COVID-19, and all of which is evidence of vaccine-related injury. **It is clear and indisputable evidence. But only if you recognize what it is you are looking at.**

**This is the problem**. It is the same problem that Charles Richet overcame in his work, with a superior ability to observe patterns and correctly assign them to specific causal relationships. (A talent, it appears, this author has in common with the late immunologist.) Charles Richet's speech, and all of his findings, are murder mystery clues that are now more than 108 years old and, from what I can see, either long forgotten or completely ignored. This is why Richet's work provided a perfect way to plan billions of perfect murders. And this mass genocide is currently succeeding because, until this very moment, no one has been knowledgeable or observant enough to put it all together, connect the dots, and come forward to expose this clever deception. There are many who suspect something is wrong with all this vaccine hysteria, but now it can be proven.

*There are many who suspect something is wrong, but now it can be proven.*

People who are believed to be dying of SARS-CoV2, aka COVID-19, are NOT dying of SARS-CoV2, or Antibody-Induced Enhancement (AIE) – which is where the really smart doctors, who know something is amiss, are being encouraged to look. Because while recognizing the potential of AIE as a causal factor is not entirely wrong, I tend to think it may be impossible to conclusively prove.

Unfortunately, for the victims of this genocide, all they can offer are complaints that the vaccine makers are well prepared to defend against, and they have done so in many cases well in advance, by quietly predicting all future vaccine injury as "possible adverse reactions" (ADR) and "side effects." But as Dr. Robert E. Willner MD, PhD. famously said in 1993, *"There is no such thing as a side effect. There are only additional direct effects."*

16

All such effects are well known to the manufacturers and they have done their level best to hide, obfuscate and outright deny every extreme ADR example, especially death, and convincingly look you in the eye and call that effect "UNRELATED." The time has come to stop this madness and save the entire world from these monsters.

## Anaphylaxis and Vaccine-Related Injury

This is what doctors and victims do not yet understand: **All severe CV-19 cases, and every single vaccine-related adverse event, are-all examples of varying degrees of anaphylaxis.**

All the related adverse reactions (ADR), especially premature death being reported as the result of a conspicuous subsequent Covid-19 infection, or following a CV-19 vaccine procedure, are all evidence of hypersensitivity to specific foreign proteins **that have been deliberately injected into the blood stream, or to specific foreign proteins that enter the blood as a result of a bio-synthetic mRNA replacement chain that instructs cells that are already within the body to express them.**

Some of these proteins may have already be present in the body, having been introduced in a previous vaccination procedures or other injectable medications. These are primary exposures. **Any CV-19 vaccine adverse event, especially death, even symptoms being mis-diagnosed and reported as Covid-19, are not separate instances of independent illness or evidence of an unknown pre-existing condition. They are symptoms that result from secondary exposures of the twin proteins that unleash varying degrees of anaphylactic response based upon their degree of specificity,** and the wide-ranging symptoms presented in each case are attributable to the unique biochemical make-up of each individual.

*Anaphylaxis Is Literally an Example of the Body Involuntarily Attempting to Commit Suicide!*

**This event is triggered by the injection, or intra-cellular genetic manufacture, of a protein that specifically matches another protein already present in the body, to which the body has previously developed allergic hypersensitivity. Anaphylaxis is literally an example of the body involuntarily attempting to commit suicide!**

Richet's work proved that every time a foreign alien protein is deliberately introduced into the blood stream, the body will respond to that invader by priming an unexpectedly strong, violent, and potentially lethal, anaphylactic immune response. **He called this the preparatory injection**. Today this is known as pathogenic priming.

Richet discovered that, immediately following the introduction of any alien foreign protein into the bloodstream, an incubation period followed. This period varied a bit in

17

humans, anywhere from 14-30 days, with the average time being 21 days. **The body will be, forever afterwards, primed to deliver this fatal anaphylactic allergic immune response anytime the same protein is reintroduced into the blood stream via injection.** All such proteins become lethal poisons which can kill in trace amounts as small as .00001ml. This amount is vanishingly small. Keep this in mind if you ever question the toxicity of ingredients in any vaccine formulation.

Every vaccine includes a whole list of them. Doctors typically scoff at such concerns, and they will explain to you that 'anti-vaxxers' are crazy when they warn of all the toxins a typical vaccine includes in its ingredient list, because the amount of any one of them is so minute it cannot possibly harm you. They are wrong. And they are ignorant of the work of Charles Richet. Test your doctor. Ask him if he even knows who Richet is.

In this book, for the first time anywhere, I will reveal the specifics of this nightmarish plan and exactly how it is supposed to work. I will show you the proof, which can be found in Richet's 1913 speech, and show you, with first-hand accounts of actual CV-19 vaccine recipients, exactly what is certain to occur when this sinister vaccine product unleashes the anaphylactic reaction that is intended to be fatal.

To my knowledge, I am the only person, outside of this eugenicist cabal, who has been able to recognize that anaphylaxis accurately describes exactly why ALL mRNA VACCINES WILL LEAVE ALL RECIPIENTS OF THEM EITHER PERMANENTLY DISABLED, TERMINALLY ILL, OR IMUNOCOMPROMISED AND SUSCEPTIBLE TO DEATH AT ANY TIME – especially the ones created to combat CV-19 and its mutations, which offer no viral immunity protection whatsoever.

## The Pandemic Was Created to Facilitate the Vaccine

The vaccine manufacturers are infested with, and openly funded by, eugenicist proponents. The true purpose of the entire pandemic hoax, and the relentless fear campaign that surrounds it, is a coercive psychological strategy that has already misled millions of people into voluntarily giving up their lives to advance this culling effort.

It is the goal of such people to selectively eliminate much of what they consider to be undesirable excess population, but they do not have any way to simply execute that many people. The people would not allow it, nor would we simply kill ourselves without encouragement. **The pandemic has been created to provide that encouragement.**

Living in a continual state of perpetual isolation, fear and hopelessness is driving many to insanity. It is a condition that is completely contrary to human nature and deprives us of things we need to survive in healthy ways, and those people acutely affected by such extended deprivations are taking their own lives by the hundreds. We are being treated as slaves and infectious farm animals while we await death. It is also why everyone in a position of authority on health matters works feverishly to keep up the appearance of trying to help us. But despite everything they do, they never seem to accomplish anything. Always new cases, always more restrictions, and they just continue to move imaginary goal posts for "getting back to normal" farther and farther into the future.

While all of the actors play their assigned roles, all of these so-called health protection practices contribute only to our physical weakness, and significantly so, such that all eventual occurrences of both severe COVID-19 or CV-19 vaccine adverse reactions, have been just shrugged off as unfortunate bad luck for which no one is responsible. And that legal cover was secured for all involved well in advance of 2020.

## All CV-19 Vaccine ADR's Are the Result of Induced Anaphylaxis

That protection is known today as *"State of Emergency Legislation"* and *"Emergency Use Authorization."* This is the only information that can potentially overturn all of that and allow us to prosecute those involved. I am asking you to bring this information to the attention of as many people as you possibly can, especially those who can most credibly use it to fight. The stakes are unimaginably high. This plan endangers the entire human race.

Summarized below are the key facts discovered by Charles Richet that are undeniably confirmed, and how they can be used *to conclusively prove* that all CV-19 vaccine ADR's are the direct result of repeated exposure to one or more specific proteins that induce mild to severe anaphylaxis in subjects due to the pre-disposed hyper-sensitivities that result when the same protein is reintroduced.

*What Richet learned was how to induce allergic hypersensitivity. This hypersensitivity is permanent. This is the eugenicists' weapon.*

Once the preparing protein has been delivered, the identical unleashing protein can be reliably found in the formulations of various common vaccines, in the CV-19 vaccine, or later expressed in the host body as a result of the mRNA they introduce. Additional evidence for this conclusion can be found in the text of Richet's 1913 Nobel Prize acceptance speech, and in the subsequent research of several others who followed him. I will frequently paraphrase and use excerpts from that speech as we go.

Richet's experiments proved that hypersensitivity was an immune phenomenon. His work in anaphylaxis helped to elucidate diseases such as hay fever and asthma, as well as others that arise from massive allergic reactions. Further analysis by other researchers demonstrated the reasons for the dual toxic effects of actinotoxin, immunogenicity and hyper-sensitizing at the same time. What Richet learned was how to induce allergic hypersensitivity. This hypersensitivity is permanent. This is the eugenicists' weapon. Richet wrote:

19

*ii"Phylaxis, a word seldom used, stands in the Greek for protection. Anaphylaxis will thus stand for the opposite. Anaphylaxis, from its Greek etymological source, therefore, means that state of an organism in which it is rendered hypersensitive, instead of being protected. To make this plain, we will consider the example of a subject that has received a poison.*

*When a subject's bloodstream is repeatedly exposed to a moderate dosage of poison via injection there are three possible outcomes:*

*The first and simplest is that there has been no change in the organism and that in receiving the same dosage as one month previously, exactly the same phenomena will result, in exactly the same conditions. Naturally, this is what happens most of the time.*

*The second possibility is that the subject has become less sensitive. In other words, the preceding intoxication has produced a certain condition of tolerance or non-sensitivity. This will mean that a stronger dose is necessary at the second injection to give the same results. This is the case of (relative) immunization.*

*The third possibility, frequently to be observed in certain conditions which I will specify, is of heightened sensitivity. The first injection, instead of protecting the organism, renders it more fragile and more susceptible. This is anaphylaxis. The second dose when injected previously even the smallest dose as low as 0.00001ml,* [an infinitesimally minute amount], *the subject will immediately show serious symptoms like vomiting, blood diarrhea, syncope, unconsciousness, asphyxia and death."* Remember these symptoms.

Richet discovered three main factors that were borne out in repeated experiments with various animal subjects. We will concern ourselves only with the specific circumstances that apply to human subjects:

1.  A subject that has had a previous injection is far more sensitive than a new subject.

2.  The symptoms characteristic of the second injection, such as the swift and total depression of the nervous system, do not in any way resemble the symptoms characterizing the first injection.

3.  On average, a 21- day period must elapse before the anaphylactic state results. This is the period of incubation. **SOUND FAMILIAR?**

The choice of 21 days is not accidental. Had Pfizer chosen 31 days, the second dose would kill almost everyone they gave it to if emergency intervention was not available to all the recipients, and distribution would be halted – like it was at one super vaccination center in California as a result of more than a few too-frequent serious and consecutive ADR's. Apparently, there were an above-average number of previously hyper-sensitized people in the line that day.

What happened? Pfizer blamed the incidents on a batch that most likely went bad due to mishandling of the vials in an outdoor environment. It doesn't matter what they said however, because it is never their fault when something bad happens. Not that they have any legal liability to concern themselves with anyway, but it looks better to say they intend to investigate it thoroughly, which is akin to a allowing a rapist to investigate his own rape case.

**The incubation period varies according to the poison used rather than according to the host subject.** This is important to recognize, and partially explains the broad range of anaphylactic response in reported ADR.

With all the possible reactions that could result from everything in the ingredient list, prescreening of vaccine participants is all vaccine providers need to do to turn someone away if they think they already had a sensitizing exposure, like from a protein in another vaccine product, such as the annual flu shot. Not that anyone would warn you necessarily, but the ability to throttle the occurrences down a bit in this way with an ADR advisory is quite possible and easily achieved. All that is needed is a subject's vaccine and medication history, something healthcare workers routinely collect.

> *"The anaphylactogen poison will be forever after be contained in the subject's blood."*
>
> – Charles R. Richet

*"Furthermore,"* according to Richet, *"instead of applying only to toxins and toxalbumins, it holds good for all proteins, whether toxic at the first injection or not."* (Toxalbumins are toxic plant proteins that disable ribosomes and thereby inhibit protein synthesis, producing severe cytotoxic effects in multiple organ systems.) *"Anaphylaxis occurs after every subsequent injection, and multiple organ failure sometime thereafter."*

21

It is here that things get really interesting. Because an anaphylactic state can also be produced by taking the blood of an anaphylactized subject and injecting it into a normal subject, Richet discovered that *"the anaphylactogen poison is an additional chemical substance produced by the subject's body that will forever after be contained in the subject's blood."* This is the pathogeny of anaphylaxis.

Because there are so many adjuvants and proteins involved in vaccine formulations, as well as other injectable solutions and medications, isolating exactly which protein a subject has become hypersensitive to can be difficult to determine, even if one knows what they are looking for, and the range of possibilities allows for considerable variation in the same subject as well as across multiple subjects.

This makes it extremely difficult for a doctor to diagnose the exact cause of any reaction. It is for this same exact reason that pharmaceutical manufacturers can claim any number of external factors or pre-existing conditions that *"could have"* been significant and using this tactic to deflect attention away from their products is a standard operating procedure.

And they tend to get away with this ruse, because doctors typically do not understand that they specifically need to look for answers in the list of proteins a subject has been parenterally exposed to previously. And while it is true that the first exposure could have happened any number of ways that I will go on to explain, it is just absurd not to immediately examine this vaccine formulation before any other possible primary exposure is even considered, because people are currently being given the same shot twice, separated by enough time to incubate an allergic hypersensitivity, and we are seeing far too many instances of severe ADR to go on looking the other way.

If one were to just look at the number of CV-19 vaccine adverse events and compare that to the number of vaccines given, the sheer number of adverse events that have been reported thus far, and the rate at which they are occurring, should have been enough to immediately put a halt to continued vaccination drives. There have never been this many serious adverse effects associated with any medication or treatment in the past, and a far less number would have been enough to take it off the market. The fact that vaccine drives have not already been halted should indicate to everyone that this overwhelming push to vaccinate everyone anyway is far more important to vaccine manufacturers than the health of CV-19 vaccine recipients.

> *Once a subject has been anaphylactized and modified in his chemical constitution, the subject can never go back to is former state. Return to normal is not possible.*

Doctors rarely suspect the vaccines because they have been assured for years that they are reasonably safe. They are not. Plenty has gone wrong with new vaccine products in the past, but when events happened, even when the same adverse result happened over and over again, doctors and victims alike were told every extreme instance was *"rare and unexpected"* and many doctors hesitate to question that. The reason for this is simple. Pharmaceutical companies spend a lot on ensuring that outcome.

One thing Richet was <u>unable</u> to determine was when, if ever, this hyper-sensitivity would diminish or pass entirely, and despite many attempts to ascertain, with any degree of certainty, a specific expectation of susceptibility in any case he studied, he finally concluded that *"Once a subject has been anaphylactized and consequently modified in his chemical constitution, the subject can never go back to his former state. **Return to normal is not possible."** he said.* An interesting and strangely prophetic choice of words to be sure. Richet went on to say *"Anaphylactic symptoms also vary to a great extent, although the differences are marked rather according to the nature of the experimental animal than according to the nature of the poison used. It is indeed worthy of note to find that* ***"the phenomena are constant, whatever the poison used."***

# Degrees of Severity

Richet described four degrees of severity that he observed when using dogs as the animal subject but, as it turns out, dogs are extremely close to humans if you compare symptoms in the various degrees of anaphylactic responses they experience. As you go on to read the personal accounts of people who have reported adverse reactions to the CV-19 vaccines **I want you to keep the list of canine symptoms in mind, because you will see them over and over again in the complaints of patients who survive the CV-19 vaccination procedure but experience mild to severe ADR.** In the cases where the patient did not survive, the cause of death in dogs, in every case, was consistently similar to what was observed in fatal CV-19 vaccine human reactions, what Richet defines as *"fourth degree anaphylaxis."*

Richet said, *"In the lightest form, the main symptom is itching."* The vast majority of ADR reports include all kinds of dermatitis and injection site inflammations.

*"The next stage in anaphylactic intensity is characterized by **itching again, but this time more violent**. This is followed, almost immediately, by various symptoms: **more rapid breathing, lowered blood pressure, faster heartbeat, vomiting, blood diarrhea and rectal tenesmus"*** (cramping rectal pain).

*"At the third degree,"* Richet said, *"**depression of the nervous system** is such that the itching has gone or almost gone. The subject has **no strength to vomit**, there is **diarrhea, blood in the stool**, the fluid passed from the rectum is often almost wholly blood."* (Take note of ADR reports that include **blood in urine and stool, bleeding from the nose, mouth, or any mucosal surface, including heavy menstrual flows** subsequent to vaccination.)

*"The **nervous symptoms often develop so suddenly and violently that there is no time for colic and diarrhea. Ataxia** follows at once,"* Richet continues. (**Ataxia** describes a **lack of muscle control or coordination of voluntary movements, such as walking or picking up objects**. A sign of an underlying condition, **ataxia can affect various movements** and create **difficulties with speech, eye movement and swallowing**.) *"**Feelings of drunken intoxication, dilated pupils**, the subject may fall to the ground, **unconscious, or unresponsive. Labored or agonized breathing** is common. The **heartbeat may be faint**, there is a **rapid and acute loss of blood pressure**. All the symptoms point to the central nervous system being the seat of severe and sudden intoxication."*

> *This brutal assault of the poison on the nervous system is what is now called anaphylactic shock.*

24

**This brutal assault of the poison on the nervous system is what is now called anaphylactic shock**. The list of more acute symptoms that Richet observed included **violent convulsions** and **paralysis**. In his animal subjects, death immediately followed. In vaccine ADR accounts, we see both progressive and permanent instances of both in those who survive, as well as **Bells Palsy**, **Guillain-Barre Syndrome**, **uncontrollable tremors, spasms and facial tics.**

Richet continued; *"Fourth degree is the most serious in which any of the symptoms displayed in lesser degrees worsen to such a point that **death occurs within hours**. Sometimes, however, a subject may briefly recover."*

This pattern of brief recovery repeats often in almost all vaccine ADR reports that end tragically. After 15 or 30 minutes of hell, some extreme symptomatic episodes may appear to have passed and the patient is allowed to go home, but they do so reporting residual complaints that may persist for days or even weeks afterwards. In reports where death is the end result, typically the stories recount people that go home and die within one to four days. More than one has passed out while driving, resulting in a fatal traffic accident. Many die alone and are only discovered later in their beds, on the floor, or sitting in a chair. Often death takes place during the night following the injection, but consistently after a period of apparent recovery.

*Sometimes, however, the patient may briefly recover. This pattern of brief recovery repeats often in almost all vaccine ADR reports that end tragically.*

This is the also a pattern that is repeated in the death reports coming from nursing and care homes where, at last count on February 12th, 2021, the rate of death following either dose of CV-19 vaccine was 54.79 percent for all people in the 75+ age group. That's more than HALF!

In the reports of injection site reactions, there are frequent accounts of something resembling tumorous masses that persist for days and weeks after, many with associated redness and other skin irritations. Nicolas Maurice Arthus, a contemporary of Richet's noticed that *"in rabbits, if both preparing and unleashing injections were given in the same spot ulcers and gangrene was commonly observed but no other symptoms."*

I am not currently aware of anyone reporting gangrene in CV-19 vaccine recipients, however reports do mention the sudden appearance of bullae, which are fluid-filled pustules and other lesions. These localized effects of anaphylaxis were often called the "Arthus phenomenon" after Nicolas Maurice Arthus, the French immunologist and physiologist who first observed it. Arthus also noted that rabbits frequently displayed respiratory conditions following injections that, in humans, would be described as **pneumonia**.

These occurrences are being frequently misdiagnosed as COVID-19 infection. As I stated earlier, COVID-19 is not its own disease. Therefore, it is inappropriate to use the term to describe any condition. Reports of people, especially the elderly, coming down with pneumonia or **persistent flu symptoms** immediately after vaccination are extremely common, as are **intense headaches, fatigue, muscle aches and pains, loss of taste, fever, chills, sweats, swollen lymph nodes and other endocrine gland sensitivity and/or swelling and general malaise**. It must be pointed out that symptoms of flu are identical to symptoms of mild anaphylaxis because to call these reactions COVID-19 is to both deny COVID-19 is flu and flu can be confused with mild anaphylaxis. It is like defining specific words as hate speech. All words are speech. Allowing the same pointless distinctions in medical diagnosis predisposes a physician to rule out certain treatments and diagnoses based on nothing, which is just poorly practiced medicine. There is a misplaced fear of blaming vaccines amongst doctors which is as insidious and serious as the misplaced fear people now have of common colds, and legitimatizing such errors can only lead to more serious errors that frequently have life-threatening consequences.

In his Nobel address, Richet also recounted the story of a doctor who had given himself a preventive injection of anti-plague serum. This doctor later tried to encourage his students to believe that this was a good idea, and to prove it was safe, he gave himself a second dose, to set an example. That second injection however had an unleashing effect and killed him two hours later. Richet went on to say, *"the effects of anaphylaxis in mankind are very well known."* Keep these facts in mind later, as you read the first-hand accounts. *"It is only in the rarest case,"* Richet said, *"that the first injection is productive of immediate reaction. When it comes to the second injection, an immediate reaction follows for 90 percent of the cases, that is to say, when the period between the first and second injection is from 10 to 30 days."*

*It is only in the rarest case that the first injection is productive of immediate reaction. When it comes to the second injection, an immediate reaction follows for 90 percent of the cases.*

The symptoms being observed are very close to symptoms Richet cited when observing his animal subjects: *"Urticaria"* (Also called the nettle rash, a disease characterized by a transient eruption of red pimples or plaques (wheals), accompanied with a burning or stinging sensation and with itching; *"Erythema"* (Erythema is a type of skin rash caused by injured or inflamed blood capillaries that usually occurs in response to a drug, disease or infection. Rash severity ranges from mild to life threatening.); *"Pangs of pain, itching, and in the worst cases **demi-syncope, with nausea, vomiting, hyperthermia, edema over the whole skin area** and **general urticaria."*** All these symptoms can be searched in public databases that record vaccine ADR, which I strongly recommend that everyone considering the vaccine look through.

On substances apt to develop the anaphylactic state, Richet distinguished between colloids and crystalloids; *"Crystalloids are on the whole non-active. I am not aware of any successful attempt to induce anaphylaxis by one crystallizable salt or by any alkaloid. On the other hand,"* he said, *"all the proteins, without exception, produce anaphylaxis, with all sera, milks, organic extracts whatsoever, all vegetable extracts, microbial proteinotoxins, yeast cells, dead microbial bodies.* **It would be of more interest now to find a protein which does not produce anaphylaxis, than to find one that does.** *"*

Proteins are the building blocks of the body and the body creates them all the time as needed. Any protein created by the body is considered "self." Any alien foreign protein that is mechanically introduced is considered by the body as "not self." It is really that simple. Vaccine antigens are alien foreign proteins. This is why vaccines elicit an immune response. In fact, all attenuated vaccines contain one or more proteins. This is what constitutes the attenuated viral material, but repeatedly introducing the same foreign protein causes hypersensitivity and the result of that second exposure is anaphylaxis. The only thing that is different about mRNA vaccines is the source of the foreign material. It is certainly not safer for this reason.

The mRNA in CV-19 vaccines are instructions that use host cells in the body to create foreign proteins. All such proteins are considered 'not self' by the body and the body attacks them all. So as a population obsessed with vaccines, we are building a lengthy list of toxins we are all hypersensitive to, to which any secondary parenteral exposure will, with complete certainty, cause some degree of anaphylaxis. The degree remember, is based upon the poison, so the closer in chemical composition a secondary exposure is to the first, namely its specificity, is what governs the severity of the reaction.

Richet explains: **"Most important of all is the degree of specificity, meaning how similar the preparatory injection is to the unleashing injection.** *For example, if the preparatory injection is of goat's milk, then the unleashing injection will be much stronger, and will have more intensive effects if made from goat's milk than if made from cow's or sheep's milk."*

Both Moderna and Pfizer have two dose vaccine products and they tell us not to mix the brands. It follows then, that they are in some way different, but exactly how they differ is something to examine more closely. Certainly, 'different' translates into 'safer' according to Richet, but we are being told to get the exact same formulation twice in a row. If all injections of specific brands of CV-19 vaccine doses are the same each time (according to the literature each dose is the same), and they are administered in two doses with 21 days in between, this is a recipe for disaster! It is not how you protect anyone. **It is how you deliberately induce anaphylaxis.** Can no one see that? If the time needed to incubate hypersensitivity in humans is 14-30 days then 21 days is right in the middle of that range, meaning that regardless of what particular protein sets off an unleashing effect, if the incubation period completes, a violent anaphylactic reaction is all but guaranteed.

Consider Russian roulette. With the first injection you play with one loaded chamber. With a second, you play with four loaded chambers. Add a third injection (as Bill Gates has recently suggested we do) very nearly the same as the either of first two, and the chances of having any empty chambers in the gun reduces to nothing. For a population reduction program to succeed, using a vaccine that killed everyone immediately after every second dose would be far too obvious a flaw in the vaccine, but at 21 days some people will surely die while others will not. Instead, you will see them present varying degrees of anaphylactic response on the second exposure from next to none all the way up to death, obviously, because the incubation period had not effectively completed in every case. But why suggest three?

> *The effects do not ever go away. They are for life.*

Is Gates unhappy with the ADR death toll? And if the incubation period that causes hyper sensitization is not completed before the second dose, this does not mean it won't complete after 30 days. In the case of mRNA vaccines subsequent injections may not even be not required, since the body is being programmed to create these unleashing proteins. They are, of course, being recommended anyway.

Remember, these sensitivities do not ever go away. They are for life. And, in the event that you have yet another CV-19 vaccination at any time down the road, because someone says later on that you need it to ensure immunity continues, or possibly due to a suggestion that it will be effective against new variants, what then?

If the formulation you receive is the same, death is far more certain to result, and we have already been told to expect lots of new vaccines for all sorts of illnesses. Every one of them is a new spin of the wheel of death, and the only one able to reliably predict, and selectively unleash a fatal anaphylactic reaction every time, is the vaccine manufacturer, who knows exactly what is in every shot and how all of them compare in terms of specificity to every other vaccine a subject is recorded to have received – something they want us to carry around with us now to leave the house or do anything in public.

You, however, by just following orders, are gambling with your life. How is it no one can see that these legally indemnified pharmaceutical companies, simply by keeping proprietary records, have acquired total control over life and death – and the people are at their mercy. If you think you can figure out with 100 percent certainty what is in any vaccine, or what proteins these mRNA sequences may express in your body's cells, I challenge you to try. You don't even speak this language. The ingredient lists in the package inserts only list adjuvants that frequently induce allergic reactions with only one exposure, but the genetic instructions encoded in these mRNA sequences are not ingredients. Even if they were to list them, such genetic sequences may as well be written in cuneiform. Individual patients do not even have any recourse for an error!

This is completely unacceptable. We can all, literally, be systematically culled from the Earth by vaccine bio-weapons without any repercussions, making coercive vaccine requirements legalized medical tyranny.

Now, I would be remiss not to mention that Richet pointed out that his results were achieved by lining up injections and exposures intentionally and, in so doing, the results became predictable. He does allow for the possibility that body chemistry could unravel some of his compounds over time, thereby allowing a subject to escape the incubation period that produces hypersensitivity, **but he never saw it happen.**

Paradoxically, is it this very thing upon which the entire concept of vaccination is based. The idea that a toxin, delivered in a weakened or inert state, can jolt the immune system just enough to insert a memory file into the immune system's enemy file cabinet without causing anything approaching severe anaphylaxis is a delicate matter. To achieve immunity without any anaphylactic response, even when consecutive booster shots are needed, well, that's quite the trick, isn't it?

We know what happens when two consecutive parenteral exposures of any foreign protein are the same and 30 days have passed between injections, so either vaccines and vaccine boosters differ just enough in their respective preparatory ingredients, or neither the shots nor the boosters that follow contain anything valuable at all, and all they have been doing with these vaccines for years is priming more and more people by making them hypersensitive to more and more compounds until some future vaccine created later unleashes a deadly reaction. Vaccine use has been commonplace for quite some time now, making it difficult to ascertain whether or not any of the ingredients contained in any previous vaccine formulation have anything to do with the eugenics experiment currently going on. We just have no way of knowing if any of them, or even all of them, were given to enable specific lethal possibilities, but given the reckless and bold moves being made today by remorseless manufacturers, it cannot be entirely ruled out.

Honestly, neither you nor I, should focus on any other attenuated vaccine right now. Only the CV-19 products. These mRNA vaccines are many orders of magnitude more dangerous because of the very manner in which they work. They pervert our precious genome, a biological blueprint that has ensured the survival of the human race for the entire time it has been on the Earth – and that is what we are being fraudulently fear-mongered and coerced to do.

You can't speak out about it; you can't ask questions. Now, you either get your vaccines or live in fear, drop out of society as an outcast, or refuse them and attempt to remain in society only to be shunned like a leper. And as people make their choices, you will see more and more examples, like the ones in this book, of vaccine recipients suddenly dropping like flies and suffering all manner of extreme inflammatory maladies over time with no one to properly address the root cause of their suffering.

It is not accidental that healthcare workers and doctors are first in line for this – not to be better able to care for you, or because of any higher likelihood that they would be exposed to a virulent pathogen, but to eliminate those with more venerable medical knowledge, and to replace them all with a new generation of pro-vaccine practitioners and even less competent robotic healthcare options that will all have "vaccine blindness." People will notice too late that there are fewer and fewer of these wise physicians to defend them, until all those unanswered questions about what is killing everyone around you becomes a very real thing to fear.

And that's not the end of it – not even close. Richet discovered passive anaphylaxis, indirect anaphylaxis, and even alimentary anaphylaxis. I will touch briefly on each one because they are important to understand – if only to speculate about how they might factor into this plan – and be combined with other things we have been told to expect whose sole purpose may be to lay even more insidious traps that hasten our demise in a similar fashion. But before I do that, let's quickly review what we know so far.

## Every Vaccine Adverse Reaction Is an Anaphylactic Response

Every vaccine adverse reaction is an example of one of the four degrees of anaphylactic response. This is the only explanation that can explain every symptom seen in every patient and physician account of something gone wrong in a CV-19 vaccine administration procedure.

And manufacturers are clearly aware of this. They even tipped their hand when they cautioned people with a history of allergic reactions to avoid these injections. But eventually, people everywhere will come up against some reason that will make them risk it. Perhaps it will be the fear of illness, or the potential loss of a job. Maybe it will be the only way out of a quarantine facility like the ones we are seeing in other countries right now, or perhaps due to the outrageous fines being levied for challenging such mandates. Many will be motivated simply by poverty. Expect to see cash incentives to get vaccinated being offered very soon.

# Methods of Inducing Anaphylaxis

| INDUCED ANAPHYLAXSIS | | | | |
|---|---|---|---|---|
| **A** | **+** | **B** | **=** | **C** |
| Preparing Injection | + | Unleashing Injection | = | Apotoxin [a new third poison] |
| **14-30 DAY INCUBATION PERIOD** | | | | |
| Initial Exposure | + | Secondary Exposure | = | A New Substance |
| Protein Toxin/Antigen | + | Protein/Toxigenin | = | (Anaphylactized Blood) |
| **First CV-19 Shot** | + (21 Days) + | Second CV-19 Shot | = | 50/50 Chance of Anaphylaxsis |

In a series of additional experiments on the process at work here, Richet was able to show several other interesting aspects of anaphylaxis.

1. He was able to inject anaphylactized blood taken from one hyper-sensitized subject into a new subject that had not been deliberately hyper-sensitized and induce a lethal allergic reaction. *"Almost harmless doses cause death within a matter of hours in dogs that had not been anaphylactized but had had injections of serum from anaphylactized animals."* He called this **passive anaphylaxis**, and if you understand how dangerous anaphylactized blood can be, it raises all kinds of questions about the possibility of lethal apotoxins potentially contaminating stocks of human blood commonly used in medical procedures.

2. He was also able to isolate the apotoxin itself and use that to induce a lethal allergic reaction in a new subject that had not been deliberately hyper-sensitized. He called this **anaphylaxis in-vitro**. All apotoxins caused an unusually extreme and violent reaction in his subjects causing death in as little as 36 hours.

   **Just look at how many deaths follow CV-19 injections, then look at the amount of time it takes for death to occur.** Are these many thousands of unique apotoxins being recorded?

3. He was even able to hyper-sensitize a subject in advance and induce a particularly violent, lethal reaction **with a food.** He called this **alimentary anaphylaxis**. This was not an easy feat. *"Such proteins would, of course, need to be highly specific, being soluble, absorbable, and resistant to fermentation in digestive fluid,"* Richet said. But consider what proteins could possibly be

31

specifically manufactured in <u>lab-grown meats</u>, and there is little more to say on the topic.

4.  **Indirect anaphylaxis** is a bit more complex and observed over two exposures of chloroform given to a dog, with a month in between shots. Richet observed severe leukocytosis that appeared a few days after the second exposure. Richet hypothesized that the unusual appearance of leukocytosis was a marker that provided evidence that the break-up of proteins in hepatic cells in the liver created a sensitizing reaction on the first exposure, and an unleashing reaction on the second. He didn't expound much on this in his address, but it is possible that any appearance of leukocytosis should be considered in the evaluation of vaccine ADR. Richet said, *"The digestive juices have powerful action, but it is probable that part of the protein escapes and certain particles pass into the circulation, thus effecting a true antigen injection, which can thus set off the leukocyte reaction. It follows that each time soluble protein is introduced by the digestive channels, anaphylactic reaction may result, as it is equivalent to an antigen injection."*

Leukocytosis is the sudden appearance of extremely high white blood cell counts that indicate the presence of abnormal inflammation. Leukocytosis itself can cause symptoms. If the number of white blood cells is high, it makes the blood so thick that it cannot flow properly. This is called hyperviscosity syndrome. It happens with leukemia, but it is rare. This is a medical emergency that can cause a **stroke, problems with vision or breathing and bleeding from mucosal areas such as the mouth, the stomach or the intestines.**

This is significant because a sudden onset of leukocytosis is evidenced by **fever and pain or other symptoms at the site of an infection; fever, easy bruising, weight loss, and night sweats** with leukemia and other cancers; **hives, itchy skin** and **rashes** from an allergic reaction on your skin, and **breathing problems** and **wheezing** from an allergic reaction in your lungs.

**Look for these symptoms in the personal accounts included in this book. These are ALL complaints reported by CV-19 vaccine recipients and the physicians that administered vaccines to them.**

I cannot possibly include them all, they number close to 26,000 at the time of this writing, but I have read many thousands of them and **symptoms corresponding to leukocytosis are listed in almost every one.**

*Richet found he could shorten the experiment and kill any subject with a single injection of an infinitesimally tiny dose.*

32

Richet made all kinds of serums from samples taken from his subjects and found he could shorten the experiment and kill any subject with a single injection of an infinitesimally tiny dose.

He also discovered that the pairs or toxins and toxigenins need not be exactly the same to cause a reaction. They could, in some cases, simply belong to the same allied protein group.

What this means is that, in his day – and possibly in ours, accurately mapping out every possible protein pairing that might cause injury or death would require a massive computational ability. Obviously in 1913, Richet did not have the benefit of the super-computers we have today, but even with them I cannot say with complete certainty that such mapping is possible. Whether it is or is not, however, is somewhat beside the point. Either situation is, in my opinion, a very bad one in which to be. Failing to assign some incorruptible independent body to the task of mapping them all means that vaccine injuries may continue to appear mysterious, but the ability to map even a few specifically selected pairings allow for the execution of an effective eugenics operation, the mechanics of which would be so subtle as to never be discovered.

Once these details like this are taken into consideration, **SUCH PATTERNS ARE NOT IMPOSSIBLE TO PROVE**. If the task of mapping out every potentially deadly protein pairing is too cumbersome or even impossible, then the either inadvertent or reckless creation of all these new undocumented apotoxins may explain every instance of vaccine injury we have seen thus far, due to the fact that the vaccine manufacturers simply will not, do not, or cannot, with any certainty, eliminate every possible potential for harm.

There is certainly no incentive for them to do so. Putting one's self in the mindset such a plan would require, it seems that selecting specifically chosen protein pairings off a predetermined list would actually be the easiest way to execute such a plan, since all such information could be concealed and protected as proprietary commercial intellectual property. Unfortunately, without a means of forcing vaccine manufacturers to turn over all such technical specifications and experimental data, the very act of introducing any alien foreign proteins into the blood will forever be a horribly dangerous procedure. In his concluding remarks, Richet acknowledged this danger.

At least from the time ancient cultures mummified their dead up until the time Richet made these discoveries, the human body has not changed all that much. Richet proved this with similar experiments that included four-thousand-year-old mummified remains, and of those results he said; *"The chemical components of the human body have undergone no great variation in the course of the last four thousand years."* The use of vaccines has changed all that, and mRNA vaccines even more so.

# Why Some Vaccine Recipients Appear to Walk Away Unharmed

It is at this point that I would expect skeptical readers to be pointing out those vaccine recipients that somehow manage to walk away from even two CV-19 injections and appear to be perfectly well. I want to be clear that I have considered how such exceptions might occur. The first and simplest explanation I can think of would be an insufficient incubation period for a hypersensitivity to set in.

In humans, Richet discovered that there is a range of 14-30 days. What distinguishes one person's personal adverse reaction experience from that of another person has to do with the unique biochemical makeup of his body, while the severity depends upon the degree of specificity of the proteins introduced in both exposures. An alternative explanation, were it to be actually happening, would represent an extreme abuse of public trust on the part of vaccine manufactures, but then this entire program is itself an extreme misuse of that trust.

Given the blatant disregard for the heath and welfare of billions of people worldwide, additional slights are reasonable to expect. If at some point a story broke that announced some batch vials were found to contain nothing but saline, I would not be all that surprised. It's not as if anyone is testing any of them before giving out injections, so such a deception might occur unnoticed. If this were going on, those people who received injections of harmless material would serve as unwitting industry advocates who would no doubt encourage those around them who might be on the fence about getting vaccinated, to believe they are not being egregiously lied to.

Many will recall the example of Tiffany Dover, a registered nurse who worked in a Tennessee hospital not far from her home in Higdon, Alabama, who infamously collapsed on live television during a publicity stunt where she was filmed on the day she received a Pfizer CV-19 vaccine. Tiffany received her vaccination on December 19th, 2020. Following the incident, Pfizer damage control was redlining in overdrive after this embarrassment, and the media was awash with everything from excuses that tested the limits of credulity, to apologetic statements by other nurses, to phony fact checkers 'correcting' and re-telling the story in a way that might mislead people to believe what they saw was anything but what it was. Media coverage of this event was a virtual blunderbuss of "move along, nothing to see here".

Despite false claims that persist, even today, that Tiffany Dover is still alive, her death was recorded in Alabama public records, confirming that she died on December 23rd, 2020. No cause of death was ever publicly disclosed. I only point out this example to illustrate the extent vaccine manufacturers will go to fraudulently influence public opinion. We have seen suspicious examples of politicians and actors doing vaccine promotions. Given the Tiffany Dover fiasco, I seriously doubt Pfizer would risk such an event twice, so I find it hard to believe any of these highly publicized stage performances involved an actual CV-19 vaccine product.

Richet stated, *"Each one of us, by our chemical make-up, above all by our blood and probably also by the protoplasm of each cell, is himself and no one else. In other words, he has a humoral personality. We all have a body of stored impressions which preclude our being confused with any other specimen of our kind. In the light of notions of immunity and of anaphylaxis, it is the humoral personality, which makes us different from other men by the chemical make-up of our humours."*

Pharmaceutical product literature discloses the fact that all vaccines contain toxic ingredients in their formulations, some of which may trigger various allergic responses with a single exposure. If a specific hypersensitivity is present, that would clearly result in a serious event, but mild allergic reactions should not be confused with anaphylactic events. It is the severe anaphylactic reactions that can be deliberately and precisely induced by simply allowing for enough time to incubate hypersensitivity that should be cause for major concern. It is difficult for any average person to know in advance what, if any, hyper-sensitizations they personally have.

*It is the severe anaphylactic reactions that can be deliberately and precisely induced by simply allowing for enough time to incubate hypersensitivity that should be cause for major concern.*

But other antigens, such as the proteins that are manufactured by host cells as a direct result of introducing a foreign mRNA sequence into a person's body, that continue to proliferate to other cells over time, is a completely different process from directly injecting whole proteins that serve as toxins and toxigenins into the bloodstream. Here, we can apply a specific statement Richet made: *"Over and above the individual differences due to diverse means of immunization, there are individual differences due to diverse anaphylactizations. One has only to think of the innumerable quantity of substances that are anaphylactizing and the substances that can immunize, and one will conclude that the chemical or humoral diversity is, so to say, unlimited with the different individuals."*

## The Collection and Cataloging of DNA Samples Will Create Vast Databases of Information to Further Tamper with the Human Genome

Companies like Moderna have already publicly stated their intent to introduce mRNA vaccine products for all kinds of illnesses, each one further tampering with the genetic makeup of human beings in a manner that creates innumerable ways in which our own immune system can be manipulated, either precisely or accidentally. These constitute genetic manipulations capable of instantly unleashing the lethal self-destructive capabilities of our own immune system. For this reason alone, this reckless adulteration of the human genome cannot be allowed to continue.

And here is where the collection and cataloging of DNA samples to create vast databases of information is cause for serious concern. This is being done with data collected by genealogy companies like 23&Me, and Ancestory.com. It is also collected in certain police investigations, but by far the most comprehensive catalog ever compiled is now being assembled through the collection of every one of these Covid test swab kits!

Make no mistake, this is exactly what is being done with that information, and there are technology contracts for such cataloging that have those capable of doing this falling over themselves to bid on. Just imagine what evil could be accomplished with such a DNA repository in which every individual's predispositions and medical trivialities are collected and recorded without their knowledge or consent and open to examination by drug makers. That should make you think about everything you get from your local **pHARM**acy.

Adding to the immediate short-term risks of anaphylaxis, other outspoken and highly credible medical professionals have offered a variety of opinions on longer-term vaccine risks that are very well supported. These are stern warnings you will have to specifically look up to learn about, because they are all being actively suppressed and heavily censored. I only mention some of these briefly here because I do feel they are credible claims that should concern anyone that manages to escape a serious anaphylactic event following a course of CV-19 inoculations. It is the opinion of tenured immunology experts like Dr. Judy Mikovits, that the real impact of these vaccines is something we will see over time, as the result of an ungoverned proliferation of cells with this modified mRNA. She alleges that in addition to a SARS spike protein, the mRNA replacement chains in CV-19 vaccine formulas also use host cells to manufacture HIVgp120 which results in an irreversible autoimmune condition and bio-synthetic syncytin-1, the result of which is sterility, miscarriages and spontaneous abortions. Her claims are echoed by other experts, **most notably Michael Yeadon, formerly the Chief Science Officer for Pfizer.**

*Additional short-term risks include sterility, miscarriages, and spontaneous abortions.*

If Dr. Mikovits is correct, and I believe she is, these inflammations will become chronic and progressive. Further evidence of this is seen in vaccine recipients that develop illnesses that cause uncontrollable tremors and paralysis. Richet commonly saw this in subjects experiencing third degree anaphylaxis, but when the symtomology of these conditions present much later, months or possibly a year after vaccination, the cause is commonly found to be from chronic inflammations that degenerate the myelin sheaths covering nerve tissues. Adding to the serious short-term risk of anaphylaxis, this slower moving infestation could mean CV-19 vaccines can potentially deliver a kind of double whammy.

That any of this is actually happening, has yet to be confirmed. However, please take note, as you read them, that reports of miscarriages and spontaneous abortions of fetal tissue, are becoming increasingly common. As for the rest of it, we may never really know, since these are aftereffects of vaccination that can appear well beyond any observation period being tracked by vaccine manufacturers. Observations periods, I would argue, that are deliberately established with intervals that are too short to collect data that would include the vaccines themselves as suspects in any such investigation.

Another danger that can be equally deadly, comes from another form of hypersensitivity that has to do with the method being employed in mRNA vaccines, where the body's own cells are used to produce biosynthetic spike protein or antigen.

The claim is that a subsequent exposure to a naturally occurring antigen, that may be found in some future corona virus mutation, will result in an immune system overreaction. We can rely on such mutations to happen. That is how the virus survives year after year, and why they continue to be an annoyance to susceptible people every flu season.

The problem arises when these two pathogens meet and the immune system over responds with a cytokine storm. This effect is being called "Antibody-Induced Enhancement," and it has been recognized by numerous credible doctors and immunologists including Dr. Sucharet Bhakdi, a retired Thai-German microbiologist; Dr. Sherry Tenpenny, a respected American osteopathic physician; Dolores Cahill, a professor at University College Dublin and a recognized international expert in this field, and Lee Merritt, who has the added distinction of being a virologist who has worked in the field of bio-weaponry. They are in agreement that massive cytokine storms can easily be lethal.

In the body, the immune systems release of a massive cytokine storm as a response to pathogenic invaders is like putting out a fire with a nuclear bomb, and the result is a wildly excessive version of a common flu illness that typically presents itself as severe respiratory distress. Examples of this illness are being seen. Currently they are simply being called COVID-19. The proper concern here is that in future flu seasons, as more cases of this type are seen, they will be labeled Covid-20, 21, and so on, rather than an event that is specifically the result of an interaction that results when mRNA technology meets nature.

What I believe we are seeing in many ADR reports should probably be considered another form of anaphylaxis. Modified mRNA are simply alien foreign proteins, therefore injecting modified mRNA into the bloodstream can induce it. By this simple logic it also follows that using foreign mRNA to create alien foreign proteins can also

37

induce it. The repeating patterns I see in both extreme COVID-19 cases, bear a strong similarity to extreme ADR reports, suggesting that the body's response to any immune system tampering follows a similar pattern. Both types of examples appear to be an extension of Charles Richet's work and it appears that vaccine makers have discovered this and decided to utilize this information to fill their coffers in collaboration with politicians that serve the eugenist proponents, thus they happily pave the way for them.

Unlike severe anaphylactic events, which occur rapidly, some of these other potential outcomes can manifest much later. It is this 'arms length' between vaccine delivery and the onset of illness that is presented by the vaccine manufacturers as proof such incidents are unrelated to their products. And this has been exactly what they claim whenever it is reported. Every time a claim has been made that associates their vaccines with an injury, their response has been to conclude that the instance was either a pre-existing condition or something that developed too long after the vaccination procedure to be related. That is why I believe the attention should be squarely focused on anaphylactic events of every level of severity, because it is a frequent and frequently immediate reaction with a traceable cause that can be confirmed.

Everything brought up by Dr. Mikovits and others are a sidebar. All their arguments are certainly relevant and represent huge concerns that should be taken seriously. However, it is my personal opinion that the relationships involved are far more biologically complex and for that reason may be significantly more difficult to prove. Given the patterns I have seen vaccine makers follow, I do not doubt these relationships exist, but challenging them on such things means playing the game on their home field where their advantage is rather strong.

While forcing the expression of foreign proteins internally certainly makes mRNA technology capable of causing cause all kinds of chronic inflammatory issues, we cannot forget that inducing hypersensitivity by repeatedly injecting any foreign protein into the bloodstream is a far simpler means of achieving the same end. This is what I see going on right now, and it is what I want you to look for in the reports and personal accounts provided here and elsewhere, because it seems to me that proving this is happening requires only that the offending proteins be isolated and identified. If they are found in the vaccine products people are being given, it is case closed for vaccine manufacturers, like matching a bullet to a gun barrel.

The truth is, that while the CV-19 vaccines are most certainly going to kill people, the pharmaceutical industry doesn't need to kill you _with_ anything really. They can now make you vulnerable to a thing that would normally be harmless, and then let you just wander about until you eventually touch it. When that eventually happens and people become sick, that creates even more opportunities to sell even more medication products. Making you ill, followed by offering you cures, especially without any legal liability, is a highly profitable business model.

What the pharmaceutical industry has done here is figured out a way to reduce the population from afar, so they are nowhere in the room when you die, and to evade detection they have front-loaded the crime scene with every possible pseudo-fact to litter it up with reasonable doubt, all of which is scientifically baseless; all of which is promoted as public health policy. All such rubbish are just childish protocols and other things that make sense to people who have no medical training and thus do not bother to question anything they are told, such as: That event wasn't caused by the vaccine; it was Covid; it was a pre-existing condition; he was asymptomatic; it was a variant; he spent 10 minutes next to another infected person; it happened too long after; too soon after; it was rare; it was extreme and unusual; it was one in a million; there's no study data to suggest; blah blah blah. Always the same weak game of spin the excuse wheel and throw a dart at it.

*Richet's work proved you can die from a fatal allegeric reaction to any protein contained in a CV-19 vaccine when exposed twice.*

To summarize, and to also avoid confusion, Richet's work proved that you can die from a fatal allergic reaction to anything contained in a CV-19 vaccine. Explanations given by the other experts I mentioned warn that you may also die, either suddenly or prematurely, from many inflammatory illnesses or even any random exposure to a commonly benign flu bug that you can become exceptionally vulnerable to in the same way you can become hypersensitized to foreign proteins that enter the bloodstream.

Anaphylaxis is the related consequence of toying with the body's natural immune system and trying to improve upon what many would call God's design. Unfortunately, well-meaning doctors, who fail to understand such risks and implications, are oftentimes made unwitting accomplices in this genocide. Because they are conditioned to trust vaccines, doctors will continue to be confounded by simple colds that seem, for some mysterious reason, to escalate out of control and result in death.

Now that you understand this, it should not surprise anyone that, to brainwashed doctors who refuse to consider the potential dangers inherent in vaccines, especially genetic vaccines, every ADR will appear to be unique. Every new flu will appear to be a lethal killer bug, and the drug manufacturers, who profit from such assumptions, will be actively encouraging those conclusions.

If they can just keep it going, these fundamental misunderstandings will perpetuate fear with pandemic after pandemic, and these new corona mutations and other sudden germ panics will take the blame for the real cause of equally sudden waves of high mortality.

Because they forget Richet, whenever it results from repeated exposure to proteins injected via future vaccines, or proteins that comprise new corona mutations which will be in some way integral to the formulations of even non-mRNA CV-19 vaccines, the cause of death, in every case, will be misdiagnosed as either COVID-'X,' or any number of other inflammatory diseases when the cause of all such examples, including death, is simply induced anaphylaxis. Exposing induced anaphylaxis is key to stopping this obscene eugenics experiment once and for all.

# The Dangers of Tinkering with the Human Genome

Richet summarized the dangers of tinkering with the genetic make up of any organism and spelled out the risks of toying with the human immune system in reckless ways. He said it best, so I will conclude with his words:

*"In the first place, anaphylaxis, like immunization, creates humoral* (Relating to bodily fluids, especially serum.) *differentiations between different individuals. A guinea-pig that is anaphylactized by horse serum will not be identical to untreated guinea-pigs nor to guinea-pigs anaphylactized by ox or dog serum. This means that over and above the due to diverse means of immunization, there are individual differences due to diverse anaphylactizations. One has only to think of the innumerable quantity of substances that are anaphylactizing and the substances that can immunize, and one will conclude that the chemical or humoral diversity is so to say unlimited with the different individuals.*

*"To be different from other members of the same species, an animal has only to receive into his blood a small quantity of alien protein which anaphylactizes him in a special way, or for a microbe to evolve in his blood which gives him immunity in a special way. In the course of some years' life span, the same organism that is unique will accumulate immunities or anaphylaxia that appertain to it, diversely grouped in diverse subjects until each one of these persons will differ from all others.*

*"Each one of us, by our chemical make-up, above all by our blood and probably also by the protoplasm of each cell, is himself and no one else. In other words, he has a humoral personality. We all know very well what the personality of the psyche is. The multiplicity and the variety of our memories make each one of us different from all other human beings. We all have a body of stored impressions which preclude our being confused with any other specimen of our kind. Nothing could be clearer than this idea of the personality in terms of psyche which stands to reason and is valid in all human conscience.*

*"Now, in the light of notions of immunity and of anaphylaxis, we can conceive of another personality in juxtaposition to the moral personality and that is the humoral personality, which makes us different from other men by the chemical make-up of our humours.*

*"This is an entirely new idea. It was thought up to now, perhaps from lack of after-thought, that with individuals of the same age, race and sex, the humors would no doubt be chemically identical. Well, it is not like that at all. Every living being, though presenting the strongest resemblances to others of his species, has his own characteristics so that he is himself and not somebody else. This means that henceforth study of the physiology of the species is no longer enough. Another physiology must be taken up, which is very difficult and barely broached, namely that of the individual.*

*"It may be asked how anaphylaxis fits in to that general law, which admits of no exceptions, that living organisms exist in an optimum state of protection.*

*"It does indeed seem absurd that an organic disposition should make beings more fragile, more susceptible to poisons, for in most cases everything in living beings seems disposed to assure them a greater power of resistance. But some reflection on the final aim of anaphylaxis will give the answer.*

*"It is in fact important that animal species are of determined chemical entity. If, following the hazard of ingestion or injection, alien proteins were found in the cellular juices as part of our humours, then the chemical make-up of beings would be modified and consequently perverted.*

*"Crystalloids dialyse through membranes and are speedily eliminated. In a few days, even in a few hours, they are completely gone. Colloids however, that no dialysis can eliminate, do not disappear once they have penetrated to the blood. They fix on cellules and end up by being integral to them.*

*"Grave danger would thus face the animal species, were they not nicely balanced in their hereditary chemical make-up. If heterogeneous substances got fixed into our cellules and definitely intermingled with our humours, that would be the end of the chemical constitution of each animal species, which is the fruit of slow evolution down the generations, and all the progress that has been achieved through selection and heredity would be lost.*

> ***There is something more important than the salvation of the person, and that is the integral preservation of the race.***

*"It does not matter much that the individual becomes more vulnerable in this regard. There is something more important than the salvation of the person and that is the integral preservation of the race.*

*"In other words, to formulate the hypothesis in somewhat abstract terms but clear ones all the same: the life of the individual is less important than the stability of the species."* (Notice here how the manner in which we are all being trained to think of 'others' before ourselves when it comes to wearing masks and getting vaccines is exactly opposite Richet's conclusions.)

*"Anaphylaxis, perhaps a sorry matter for the individual, is necessary to the species, often to the detriment of the individual. The individual may perish, it does not matter. The species must at any time keep its organic integrity intact. Anaphylaxis defends the species against the peril of adulteration.*

*"We are so constituted that we can never receive other proteins into the blood than those that have been modified by digestive juices. Every time alien protein penetrates by effraction, the organism suffers and becomes resistant. This resistance lies in increased sensitivity, a sort of revolt against the second parenteral injection which would be fatal. At the first injection, the organism was taken by surprise and did not resist. At the second injection, the organism mans its defenses and answers by the anaphylactic shock."*

*"Seen in these terms, anaphylaxis is a universal defense mechanism against the penetration of heterogeneous substances in the blood, whence they can not be eliminated."* [iii]

-----

*"An optimum state of protection."* In other words; no vaccines needed.

*"If heterogeneous substances got fixed into our cellules and definitely intermingled with our humours, that would be the end..."* This is what we are being told mRNA vaccines do.

*"... the organism mans its defenses and answers by the anaphylactic shock."*
Sorry, Grandma. It wasn't me that killed you.

# It's ALL Anaphylaxis!

While it is understood that vaccine recipients include people with all manner of pre-existing conditions that impact the severity of an anaphylactic response, none of them should be confused with the onset of any anaphylactic reaction immediately following a CV-19 vaccination procedure.

*"The effects of anaphylaxis in mankind are very well known." "It is only in the rarest cases that the first injection is productive of immediate reaction. When it comes to the second injection, an immediate reaction follows for **90 percent** of the cases."*
*– Charles Richet*

**COVID vaccine adverse reactions <u>do not</u> have multiple causes.
There is only one reaction. Just one. It is all . . .
<u>Anaphylaxis!</u>**

The personal accounts that follow are grouped by levels of severity, taking into account both Charles Richet's experimental observations, as well as modern day definitions of anaphylactic severity[iv]

*"Any study of acute allergic reactions is limited by the lack of a diagnostic gold standard or widely accepted definition of anaphylaxis."*
- Simon G. A. Brown, MBBS, FACEM, PhDa,

*Simon continued, "When carefully observed,"* Brown continued, *"virtually all episodes of anaphylaxis appear to have some degree of skin involvement, although this may consist of only mild erythema and can be easily missed or go undocumented as is likely to have been the case in this study. With this in mind, the following clinical definition of anaphylaxis is proposed: Multiple-organ hypersensitivity characterized by the presence of significant gastrointestinal, respiratory, or cardiovascular involvement (nausea, vomiting, abdominal pain, throat or chest tightness, breathlessness, wheeze, stridor, hypotension, hypoxia, confusion, collapse, loss of consciousness, or incontinence) in addition to skin features (erythema, urticaria, or angioedema). Skin features may be transient, subtle, and therefore easily missed, in which case anaphylaxis may still be diagnosed if there is an otherwise typical presentation, especially where this follows exposure to a known precipitant."* **In the case of CV-19 vaccinations the precipitant is known. It is the vaccine itself!"**

I have also included groupings that bring up additional reasons for concern as CV-19 vaccines continue to roll out, such as:
- Pregnancy-, Fertility, Menstrual and Breast Feeding-related ADR.
- Compromised healthcare worker errors.
- Extreme ADR reported in VAERS, the medical database maintained by CDC to track CV-19 vaccine adverse reactions.
- Deceptive reporting practices and industry pressure to NOT report ADR.

### TOTAL CV-19 Vaccine ADR:

The February 18, 2021 release of VAERS data [3] found 19,724 cases of CV-19 Vaccine ADR.

ᚹᚹᚹ

# Covid-19 Vaccines

### and

# Induced Anaphylaxis

## Are You Questioning Whether Or Not To Take The Covid-19 Vaccine?

Before you do, get the facts on the only real cause of the Adverse Reactions...

## Anaphylaxis

by

## J. E. Lukach

# Personal Accounts and VAERS Reports

VAERS is the medical database maintained by Centers for Disease Control and Prevention (CDC) to track CV-19 vaccine adverse reactions.

# First Degree Anaphylaxis

Existing grading systems for acute systemic hypersensitivity reactions vary considerably, have a number of deficiencies, and lack a consistent definition of anaphylaxis. Some common definitions provided below:

**As defined by Charles Richet:**

> *"In the lightest form, the main symptom is itching. May also include "Pangs of pain, itching, and in the worst cases demi-syncope, with nausea, vomiting, hyperthermia, edema over the whole skin area and general urticaria."*

**Modern-day definition by Simon G. A. Brown:[v]**

> *"Reactions limited to the skin, i.e., urticaria, erythema and angioedema, defined as mild."*

*Angioedema is a swelling that occurs when fluids leave the blood vessels and enter the tissues. While angioedema can occur in any "loose" tissue in the body, but the term is usually used to describe a swelling of the face, lips, mouth, and the internal structures of the throat.*

*Erythema is redness of the skin or mucous membranes, caused by hyperemia in superficial capillaries.*

*Generally Accepted Definition based upon presentation of symptoms:*

*Includes all varieties of dermatitis, injection site inflammations, urticaria, hives, nettle rash which is (characterized by transient eruption of red pimples or plaques (wheals) accompanied by a burning or stinging sensation with itching), Erythema (inflamed blood vessels of capillaries), swellings in the skin.*

***All symptoms can be searched in public databases that record vaccine ADR. I strongly recommend that everyone considering the vaccine, review the data contained in these databases.***

What follows are first-hand accounts of the reactions experienced by those who took the vaccine, or witnessed the effects of the vaccine in family members or friends. Included are photos, personal accounts, social media posts, and other publicly posted descriptions, as well as information culled from the VAERS database, the official database of the Centers for Disease Control (CDC).

r/CovidVaccinated · Posted by u/cpys0522 5 hours ago

### 27M Modern shot 1/16

I took my first does 1/16 and felt pretty normal typical arm soreness and such but that was it. I was up pretty late and I'd say around 2am on 1/17 I started getting chills and a fever. Arm soreness became more and more painful and I woke up feeling horrible on 1/1 with fever, chills, arm soreness, pain in my arm, etc and continued throughout the day. I actually had to call out of work because it's gotten so bad. On top of the injection soreness I have this almost arthritic pain shooting down both my arms and wrists, pain in the back of my neck, and general fatigue. Really regretting taking this vaccine so quickly.

 **CarlosnRaquel Dibble**
January 6 at 6:00 AM · 🌐    ...

COVID-19 vaccine #2 symptom update as promised.

Why am I awake at 0400 you ask?  Well because I haven't been able to sleep because, I am freezing, shaking, fever 101.86, dizzy, whole body aches, painful skin, palpitations, pounding headache(like a migraine), swollen lymph nodes, and my arm feels like I've been punched with brass knuckles.  I just took some Tylenol and Celebrex hoping that I feel good enough to get up at 0700 to go to work😊.

Carlos got a mild headache last night, chest tightness (like when you are
Coming down with a cold), a little dizzy , sensitive skin, and his arm is only a little sore. 😊 not fair!

😮😆👍 74                                56 Comments  1 Share

 r/CovidVaccinated · Posted by u/KodakArab 54 minutes ago

### blood nose constantly after 2nd dose of Pfizer vaccine

 i have had a blood nose for about a week now after receiving the 2nd dose of the Pfizer vaccine. Is this a normal side effect? or should I call my GP?

well I didn't want to post this because I don't want people to make comments but I am experiencing some side effects. The vaccine hurt, as soon as she started injecting the vaccine I had burning and shooting pain. About 20-30 minutes after the vaccine I became very dizzy and lightheaded. I eventually got home and felt fine, I barely had any pain . I woke up around 2am-ish with burning unbearable pain in my arm and I had a slight fever . I took ibuprofen and put my heating pad on and eventually fell asleep. I woke up this morning to get ready for work and my face was so swollen, my arm pain still unbearable and still running a slight fever . So I called out . My face swelling is down now but my eyes are swollen and red, I feel like I have a bunch of styes starting. So I'm just resting with my heating pad . 🔒

October 31 at 4:42 PM · 🌐

My husband and I are both in the Moderna trial. Two weeks after our second shots my husband started having serious symptoms, shooting pains in extremities, extreme skin sensitivity, fatigue, serious headache, ED, nausea, cough and loss of strength. An adverse event has been submitted by the trial Doctor. Although we have no evidence to associate the two he is normally a fit and healthy guy. If anyone else has any issues please let me know, here or on IM if you prefer. Thanks.

**Dr-Cynthia Foster**
Don't take the COvid vaccine. My friend's daughter is a Physician's assistant at a New York hospital. One of her fellow PA's was vaccinated with the new COvid vaccine and had an extreme allergic reaction called Stevens Johnson Syndrome. It makes all the skin on your body peel off and makes you go blind. She looks like a burn victim and is now in the burn unit with her eyes taped shut and they don't know if she will survive. If she does, she will likely be blind in at least one eye (if not both) and have to go through numerous skin graft surgeries and be scarred all over her body for life. In terms of an adverse reaction to something, this is as bad as it gets. Please do an Internet search on Stevens Johnson's Syndrome so that you know how bad this is. I may post a pic later. This is an absolute real story and really horrifying.

**Locklyn Lamb** shared her first post.
· 5 hrs · 🌐

I got the first round of the moderna vaccine on Wednesday-, I didn't have any reaction immediately, but later that night, my neck / throat broke out in hives and was super itchy- benadryl knocked it out. My arm wasn't sore, except when I touched it after about 24 hours from the time I got the shot!

 cv19vaccinereactions   ···

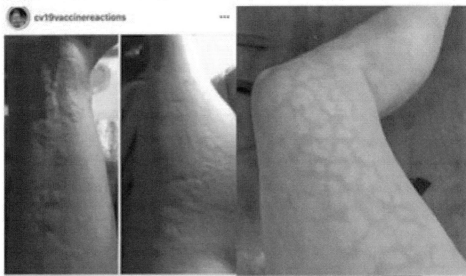

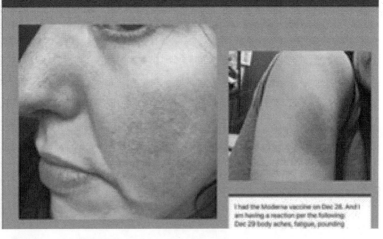

I had the Moderna vaccine on Dec 28. And I am having a reaction per the following:
Dec 29 body aches, fatigue, pounding

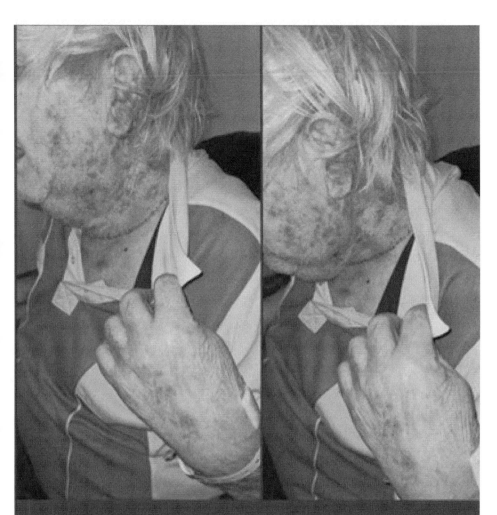

**Kathleen Connors**
January 23 at 7:02 AM · 🌐

My grand father Jack donoghue had the pizer vaccine last saturday since he had he broke out with a rash on one side of his body the side he had the vaccine and been to hospital twice and the doctors don't no wants wrong with him they think it's allegreic reaction but they don't no he can bearly talk and walk he's in a bad way all since he had the vaccine

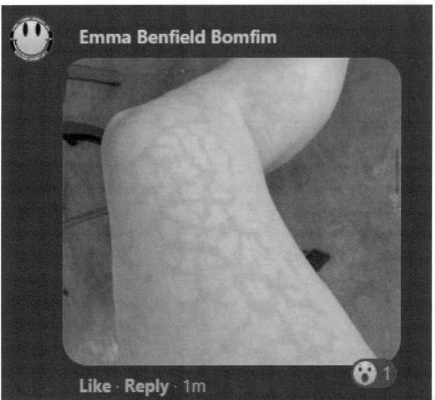

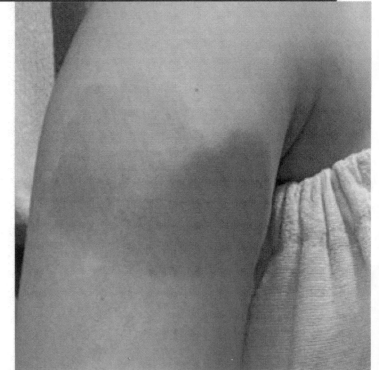

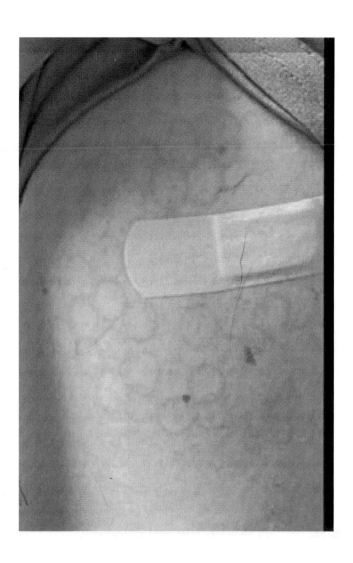

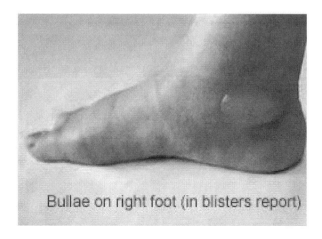

Bullae on right foot (in blisters report)

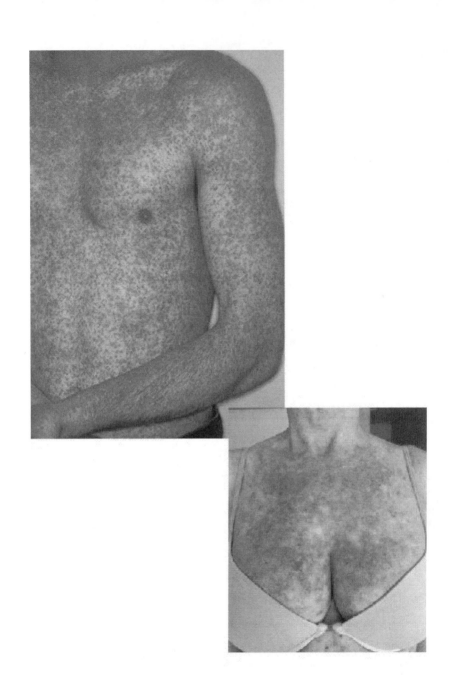

"Morbilliform Rash"

# Case Descriptions Below From VAERS Database

**BLISTERS - From the 2/18/2021 release of VAERS data:**
Found: <u>22 cases</u> where Vaccine targets COVID-19 (COVID19)
Manufacturer:  PFIZER/BIONTECH; Symptom: Blister

**Write-up:** Swollen lymph nodes with lesions and blisters

**Write-up:** Blisters around hips, thighs, and elbows.

**Write-up:** Exactly a week later, developed blisters (almost like herpes like) on the R side of my nose and on the inside of my nose. I never had blisters in my life, or herpes like **blisters on my face**. Now on 1/5/21, the blisters are starting to dry, but are still there.

**Write-up:** 8 Days after vaccination: **Painful fluid filled bumps** in a linear formation discovered this morning

**Write-up:** experienced body rash and little **blister sores** on her body and both arms, swelling of eyes and rash beneath eyes. The events resulted in doctor or other healthcare professional office/clinic visit.

**Write-up:** 3 hours after patient received vaccine on 12/27/2020 @ 2pm she started to feel flushed in the face and hands. She also started to get **blisters** on both hands.

**Write-up:** Presented from clinic with 3-4 days of extensive rash. There were multiple areas **of skin sloughing** on bilateral upper extremities and abdominal wall.

**Write-up:** Days after vaccination: 3. Started out as possible eczema, **blisters throughout groin** and perineal area, nodes in groin were very swollen and tender, also had flu-like symptoms. Patient was seen in the Emergency Department and treated.

**Write-up:** Very pruritic maculopapular -purple and red rash diffusely throughout body and extremities and neck. **Sores in the mouth and blisters forming on palms** of hands and soles of feet with some pain, ureteral meatus erythema and anal erythema. pain with swallowing.

**Write-up:** 2 hrs after 2nd injection, felt like I was burning from inside out; skin red; flushed; rash; scratch throat; body aches; dizziness; headache; lymph nodes tender; eye swelling; blurred vision; blisters on the trunk of my body as well as lips and gums; tooth pain; jaw pain; I also had leg and bilateral foot pain x 4 days; **all my mucous membranes were red, irritated and blistered;**

**Write-up:** Days after vaccination: 11. Diagnostic Lab Data: Surgical Pathology reports: FINAL DIAGNOSIS: SKIN, RIGHT THIGH, BIOPSY: **SUBEPIDERMAL BULLAE WITH EXTENSIVE EPIDERMAL NECROSIS** AND MIXED INFLAMMATORY INFILTRATE. NO EVIDENCE OF MALIGNANCY. Comment: The clinical concern for toxic epidermal necrolysis is noted, and the histologic findings support this impression. Extensive subepidermal **bullous formation** with associated mixed inflammatory infiltrate composed of neutrophils, eosinophils, and lymphocytes is noted in the larger of the two skin fragments, while the smaller fragment shows diffuse epidermal necrosis.

**Write-up:** Bilateral ears because hot, red, swollen, **blistered, and painful** approximately 1 hour and 20 minutes after vaccine was administered.

**Write-up:** The night of the 18th my right eye was bothering me so I was itching it in my sleep, when I woke up on the 19th my eye was red and I thought I had injured it in the night and it bothered me all day but I didn't get it checked, I went to urgent care the 20th because I noticed there were **vesicles on my right eye.**

**Write-up:** Surface blisters, blistering rash all over; Hives; Itchy tongue; Headache; A 44-year-old female patient received the first dose of BNT162B2 a single dose for COVID-19 immunization. After receiving the vaccine, patient had hives and an itchy tongue . Patient received some Benadryl at site. She spoke for about two hours and it seemed to ease a little bit. Patient came home and slept a quite a bit. As soon as she woke up, patient had the itchy tongue and hives again, so she took another the Benadryl. She woke up and then had a **blistering rash all over. But the blisters were like deep blisters all over her body.**

---

**VAERS ID:   1028885**

Write-up: **Patient (now deceased)** received 1st dose of Pfizer-BioNTech vaccine around December 21, 2020 and was **noticed to be scratching**, fatigued, and unresponsive by a family member on December 24, 2020. He received the second dose of the same vaccine around January 22, 2021. **Pockmarks and bleeding scratch marks were noted by a family** member on the patient's face prior to this second dose. On January 28, 2021 a family member was alerted that the patient was suffering from **severe bullous pemphigoid**- a skin condition that has never been experienced by the patient, has been reported to be **related to COVID-19 viral infection, and to T-cell responses promoted by vaccines. A corticosteroid was given, but did not work. Blisters developed to the point hands had to be dressed.**

# Second Degree Anaphylaxis

Existing grading systems for acute systemic hypersensitivity reactions vary considerably, have a number of deficiencies, and lack a consistent definition of anaphylaxis. Some common definitions provided below:

**As defined by Charles Richet:**

> *"The next stage in anaphylactic intensity is characterized by itching again, but this time more violent. This is followed, almost immediately, by various symptoms: more rapid breathing, lowered blood pressure, faster heartbeat, vomiting, blood diarrhea and rectal tenesmus"* (cramping rectal pain).

**Modern-day definition by Simon G. A. Brown:**

> *"Diaphoresis, vomiting, presyncope, dyspnea, stridor, wheeze, chest/throat tightness, nausea, vomiting, and abdominal pain had weaker, albeit significant, associations and were used to define moderate reactions."*

> *Diaphoresis is perspiration.*
> *Presyncope is a state of lightheadedness, muscular weakness, blurred vision, or feeling faint.*
> *Stridor* is airway obstruction.

**Generally Accepted Definition based upon presentation of symptoms:**

> *More rapid breathing, lowered blood pressure, faster heartbeat, vomiting, blood diarrhea and cramping.*

**All symptoms can be searched in public databases that record vaccine ADR. I strongly recommend that everyone considering the vaccine, review the data contained in these databases.**

# Case Descriptions Below From VAERS Database

> I went to work today and ended up in the ER. Thank god I work at a hospital. I'm positive this episode is from the Covid19 vaccine. I had tachycardia. My heart beat was 239. I haven't felt right since I got the injection on Tuesday. I have had a headache ever since. I will not be getting the 2nd shot. This was my experience with the vaccine I felt I should share it.

---

**VAERS ID:1000654**

Age: 58.0  Sex: Female  **Days after vaccination:  9**

Symptoms: Abdominal pain, Body temperature increased, Chills, Faeces discolored, Fatigue, Haematochezia, Headache, Mucous stools, Rectal tenesmus

Write-up: white mucous stools with blood; abdominal pain; tenesmus; white mucous stools with blood; fatigue; chills; headache. a possible contributory role of the **suspect BNT162B2 in triggering the onset of blood stool cannot be excluded.**

---

**VAERS ID:  1000654**

Age: 58.0  Sex: Female  **Days after vaccination:  9**

Symptoms: Abdominal pain, Body temperature increased, Chills, Faeces discolored, Fatigue, Haematochezia, Headache, Mucous stools, Rectal tenesmus

Write-up: white mucous stools with blood; abdominal pain; tenesmus; white mucous stools with blood; fatigue; chills; headache. **a possible contributory role of the suspect BNT162B2 in triggering the onset of blood stool cannot be excluded.**

---

**BLOOD DISCHARGE - From the 2/18/2021 release of VAERS data:**

*Found 11 cases where Vaccine targets COVID-19 (COVID19) and Manufacturer is PFIZER/BIONTECH and Symptom is Blood* urine present or Bloody airway discharge or Bloody discharge.

# Third Degree Anaphylaxis

Existing grading systems for acute systemic hypersensitivity reactions vary considerably, have a number of deficiencies, and lack a consistent definition of anaphylaxis. Some common definitions provided below:

**As defined by Charles Richet:**

> *"Depression of the nervous system is such that the itching has gone or almost gone. The subject has no strength to vomit, diarrhea, blood in the stool, often almost wholly blood. heavy menstrual flows, nervous symptoms often develop so suddenly and violently that there is no time for colic and diarrhea. Ataxia follows at once. Feelings of drunken intoxication, dilated pupils, the subject may fall to the ground, unconsciousness, or unresponsiveness. Labored or agonized breathing, faint heartbeat, rapid and acute loss of blood pressure. violent convulsions and paralysis. Possible death immediately following."*

Ataxia describes a lack of muscle control or coordination of voluntary movements, such as walking or picking up objects, uncontrollable tremors, facial tics, difficulties with speech, eye movement and swallowing.

**Modern day definition by Simon G. A. Brown:**

> "Severe (hypoxia, hypotension, or neurologic compromise) Confusion, collapse, unconsciousness, and incontinence were strongly associated with hypotension and hypoxia and were used to define severe reactions."

Hypotension is low blood pressure.
Hypoxia is oxygen deprivation.

**Generally Accepted Definition based upon presentation of symptoms:**

All of the above including Guillain–Barré syndrome and Bells Palsy

*All symptoms can be searched in public databases that record vaccine ADR. I strongly recommend that everyone considering the vaccine, review the data contained in these databases.*

**Fighting4Freedom** @yattypat · 2m     ···

Sharing from FB.

I will tell you what happened to my Dad. He **died** last Tuesday. No underlying health problems and 100% fit. Day 4 after Pfizer **vaccine** he got double vision. It wouldn't shift so my Mum took him to A & E. CT scan of his head, showed no problems. Full MRI

**Veronica Meadows** @Veronic53583078 · 5h

Replying to @zerohedge

I am in CA and my **grandparents** were forcibly vaccinated against their will in their nursing home and now, my grandma is dying. Do NOT allow your loved ones to take this **vaccine**! Please, for the love of God. I am begging you. It's NOT safe!!!

**Taylor** 🦋 @I_Am_TaylorJ · 37m     ···

- One of my moms friends nephew just **died** from the COVID **vaccine**! People are getting the **vaccine** and dying days later from it! Absolutely NOT getting that shit EVER!

  ○ 1        ↑↓ 1        ♥ 2        ⬆

     👍 New member · 2 d · 🖼

**Violet Flame**
Yesterday at 3.22 PM · 🌐

Absolutely Heartbroken 😭😢

Please think about taking this covid-19 vaccine!!! I mean really really think!!! I know some don't understand or want to listen and the MSM is really playing on fear right now!! But We as a family are heartbroken right now, with the Death of my partners & little boys Great/Grandad yesterday!! He had the vaccine the week before Christmas, started to feel ill within days, had a fall on the 2nd January, was taken to hospital on the 3rd, felt perky on 5th, then Died on the 7th!! 16days after getting his first dose of this new covid-19 vaccination!!😢😢 They should never have been allowed to be given to anyone at all!! Having been this rushed and having no human trials!!!

Just to make ppl aware as fb took my posts down my dad had the covid vaccine and took very seriously ill after it he has had a serious reaction to it like many others I have spoke to now around the world his body can not stay still for one second to allow him to rest it's agony as it's constantly jerking like convulsions I have never in my life seen anything like this the hospital said they can't help as they don't know what this vaccine causes yet so we are stuck my poor dad suffered also with mini stroke also or stroke

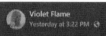

**Heather Lyons** is with **Tim Lyons**.
January 8 at 5:46 PM · 🌐

Thank you all for the text, calls and messages!!!

6 hours later and my reaction is fading. Ive had IV meds to calm my system.. Ive went Afib, tachycardia ( both confirmed by ekg), red, skin on fire, swollen eyes and felt plain miserable!!!

I should have listened to my first thought and passed on the vaccine.. for some its great for some its NOT! Dont let the media... people.. or anything talk you into something you have doubts on.. stick with your gut and go with it.... only you know your body!

As far as the 2nd one.. NOPE! Today has been horrible!

Just for note this was my first dose of the Pfizer vaccine.. I do have underlying medical conditions. POTs, MCAS, and Small fiber Neuropathy all a form of Dysautonomia.. but was told that the vaccine is better then Covid (which our house already had and recovered well from ) .

After the vaccine was administered I walked away maybe 50' and I started to feel dizzy I felt light headed and as if I was drunk my legs feel real week they took me outside so I could catch some fridge fresh air and they set me down on a chair I was very dizzy my legs and my knees felt like I couldn't stand up and they were very weak I kept seeing a the rails double vision and I started to have a tightness in the back of my neck I felt they warrant come over my head and my forehead got very very cold And then I felt as I was gonna blackout and pass out and I was gasping for air and suddenly my tongue went into a spasm and it went to the top of my the roof of my Roof of my mouth and I couldn't breathe and I was able to send a message for someone to come and help me as I was sitting there by myself they rushed over by now looking at my text message it was for 02 which was within 15 minutes of the vaccine when I had my 1st episode and then minutes after that 3 more came with the same oh unable to swallow I lost the ability to swallow and my tongue fell like I had no control it was just automatically stuck to the roof of my mouth.. Upon the arrival of Ems I was told there was no treatment and there was nothing they could do told me to wait 24 to 48 hours in the symptoms should subside it's been over 72 hours in the symptoms are still occurring. I continue to feel dizzy light headed and now have high blood pressure which was not present before visit ER prescriptions for steroids with issued, I Told to go home and rest. Followed up with family doctor in the morning and was told it was not an allergic anaphylactic reaction probably more so neurologically ransom blood tests waiting for results continue to have loss of control over tounge spasms unable to eat Accompanied by fatigue dizziness and high blood pressure

I started having chills before bed 12 hours after receiving vaccine. I woke up late morning (now 24 hours later)with a terrible migraine and continued to have chills. I went to the bathroom after I woke up and felt very nauseated and sick. I then started seeing black dots and felt very dizzy. Soon after my vision went completely black for what seemed to be about 5 min. I was shaking, having difficulty breathing and fell to the ground. My fiancé called 911 and an ambulance was on its way. The EMTs showed up and took my vitals. At this point I was able to see again and was sitting down. My blood sugar was normal along with my oxygen stats. My blood pressure was low while sitting and standing. I was starting to feel better and didn?t end up going to the hospital. I continue to have chills, body aches and a headache but so far no more blackening out episodes. It was the scariest experience of my life!

24 hours after receiving the Covid-19 vaccine, a 23-year-old man developed a rare multisystem inflammatory syndrome, which causes, among other things, severe damage to heart function.

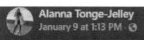

**Alanna Tonge-Jelley**
January 9 at 1:13 PM · 🌐

Before I start this post I am in no way feeding into conspiracies, lies etc this is from true experience and i am currently having to write this with one hand. Today I went in for my pfizer covid 19 vaccination because i work in a care home and thought it would be in best interest of my residents to have it i was offered a choice! before i had the jab i was asked if i had any allergies which i stated a mild egg allergy so after my jab i was told to stay for a 30 minute observation to see if the vaccine caused a anaphylactic reaction. I was fine apart from a mild headache i put that down to not eating properly when i got home i decided to go for a nap which lasted an hour little did i know everything was going to get worse. When i woke up i could barely feel my right side (i was vaccinated in my right arm) and could barely string a sentence together i had slurred speech and little energy. as time went on i lost complete sensation in my right arm and leg and my headache became an excruciating pain in my neck aswell, my mum suspected something was wrong and called 111 for some advice as we weren't sure if these are normal side effects. When speaking to 111 they sent an ambulance which came in 10 minutes, i was assessed and sent to the royal hospital i was then sent for a CT scan and admitted as a potential stroke bearing in mind i am 19 years old. the CT scan was clear but there was no explanation for the loss of feeling in my body I am now on a stroke ward despite no sign of a stroke to monitor if my feeling comes back and to see if i can walk again.
So please unless you need this vaccination refrain from getting it because we all know what is the reason i am in this state right now but they refuse to say it!
UPDATE. i put this post for awareness not to be trolled and called a liar when i am currently unable to even go to the toilet without full assistance today i managed to take a step using the whole strength in my body. i would never lie about something so serious.
I'd like to add another update and progress video as no i don't think i have to prove myself but just show the seriousness of my situation. This video was during my therapy session on trying to get my arm moving again i used all the strength i have to try and move a fork to my mouth. I have not once said anti vaccine etc i decided to take it i simply just shared what has happened to me.

🅱️🅱️ @TrizzyTraap · 52m     ...

I can't stress this enough ! Please don't take Covid-19 **Vaccine** my aunt took it and had complications that resulted I her being brain **dead** but by the grace of god she made out of surgery and is on the road to recovery. But let that be a eye opener

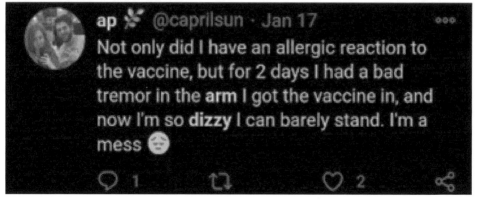

My dad had the vaccine 10 days ago
and is so so ill he has never stopped
continuously shaking and twitching
jerking he is so exhausted not slept in
10 days has anyone got any advice pls

**COVID 19 trial vaccine recipients**

1 wk  Like  Reply  More

**Carlina Wiese**

I am on this study too and after the second
vaccine in September, about 25 days later I
developed a head tremor and it has been
getting worse to where now I am having
balance issues .

on Tue  Like  Reply  More

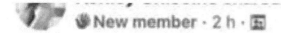
I'm a 21 year old CNA at a nurs home i was working and completely healthy i got told to go get the vaccine (from peer pressure bc i didn't want it) talk to a lady told her i had seizures in the past i had a cold and have allergies to shellfish amoxicillin and penicillin (SHE CROSSED THEM OFF AND PUT N/A! ON MY CONECENT FORM!) I took the vaccine at the 12:02 on Jan 8 i walk around and made my way to my seat and immediately felt my heart racing getting hot and dizzy i tried everything to calm my heart down and nothing worked i put a cold water bottle on my head and watched my Apple Watch to see how high my heart rate was it was 176 when i checked that's when i new something was wrong i stood up to get help and i just collapsed. I couldn't move after my hands and legs seemed paralyzed my left side of my face was all pins and needles feeling. They say i had two seizure like eps i was throwing up and screaming in pain. I then had two epi pens in the left leg i couldn't feel it at all Bc my legs couldn't feel anything my legs where completely numb and well paralyzed the emts came i was extremely tired and weak and hurt everywhere. Half way through i gained movement in the first three fingers in both hands and then the left was very delayed i still had pins and needles feeling i could feel my legs in the er  but i didn't no i couldn't move them much i gained pins and

**Krystal Anne Connelly**
Jan 25 at 3:05 PM · 🌐

Thursday 1/21/2021 I got the moderna Covid-19 vaccine , Like many people in the healthcare field I got it for my community. I work in a doctors office that has seen a high number of cases and I wanted to make sure even though I am healthy that anybody around me would be healthy too and not risk me being a carrier and giving it to them. this backfired terribly for me I got the vaccine at 10:30 AM and by 3:000pm I was having extreme pain in my right arm, slurred speech, facial numbness and weakness, headache and pressure behind my right eye. We called an ambulance because I honestly thought I was having a stroke. By the time we got settled at the hospital I was completely paralyzed on my right side of my body unable to move my arm or leg. This nightmare went on and I had several test or include CT scans two MRIs and a lumbar puncture all which came back normal minus a few things they saw on the MRIs. I've been in the hospital since Thursday and every doctor I see is just so confused on what went wrong and tells me to keep my head up but there is not enough research for them to make a definite diagnosis and that it was a new vaccine and so this is one of the problems that they predicted would happen.

**Whitney Mae** ▸ COVID 19 trial vaccine recipients

3 hrs ·

Hi guys! Just joined this page. In moderna with meridian research. Got first vaccine July 27 and second August 26. Both times I had a very sore arm, tender to touch, fatigue, body aches and headache for about 2 days. First vaccine was worse then the second. I was able to carry on most daily activities but took OTC meds and went to bed early. I have also had some ongoing mild moderate fatigue and body aches since the first one. I am not sure if it's related. I am getting more testing and blood work on Monday. Also 4 weeks ago I had gross hematuria (my urine was red) and found to have hydronephrosis (swelling or fluid build up around kidneys) without a stone or infection. So I'm getting worked up for that too. I have had my antibodies tested and did have antibodies and before I did not. So I guess we will see.

I got super hot first and then my heart felt like it was bout to come out my chest. They quickly moved me to a private location so nobody has a panic attack from watching me 😂 then I was having trouble breathing and my tongue was swelling and I had stridor. Then I was slurring my speech got nauseous and they did a neuro check on my and my left eye wasnt reacting like my right. My HR and BP were high but I refused to see what it was. I was 160 on HR though. And I was shaking like crazy even though i was super hot

3h   Like   Reply                    6 😢

## Case Description Below From VAERS Database

**Write-up:** Day 1: palpitations, dizziness Day 2: headache, redness, swelling, itching on vaccination site; GI disturbance Day 3: vaccination arm had paresthesia, heaviness, almost stroke-like symptoms; the symptoms started suddenly ** treated in the ER; IV steroids- for possible allergic reaction; tpa- for the stroke-like signs; halfway through the tpa, I felt an improvement with the arm

# Fourth Degree Anaphylaxis

Existing grading systems for acute systemic hypersensitivity reactions vary considerably, have a number of deficiencies, and lack a consistent definition of anaphylaxis. Some common definitions provided below:

**As defined by Charles Richet:**

*"Death occurs within hours of administering the vaccine. Sometimes however a subject may briefly recover."*

**Modern-day definition by Simon G. A. Brown:**

Not defined.

**Generally Accepted Definition based upon presentation of symptoms:**

Not defined.

**All symptoms can be searched in public databases that record vaccine ADR. I strongly recommend that everyone considering the vaccine, review the data contained in these databases.**

Examples in this section are taken from online social media posts.

**DaveX** @buzzconstruct · 5h

Replying to @VictorMeldrew69 and @Lesqueenb

**My** gran had a stoke 2 hours after pfizer **vaccine** Tuesday she **died**. **My** wife works in a care home same happening there having stokes after the **vaccine**. Classed as a stroke death though

I wanna say this on Infinity's platform. My sister works in the medical field in Connecticut they got the vaccinations in my sister did not get hers. Her friend did and died less then 8 hours later. They aren't announcing it. This is going to be happening everywhere I've heard accounts in Italy of deaths as well. We have to share information as a community to get a real feel of what's happening out there. Share this story get it out

12:19 AM

Omg they just found my aunt dead!

12:20 AM

She was one of the nurse got the covid vaccine tod her job & they just found dead

Seen

I am freaking tf out

so bad

Me too. My mom doesn't want her name released to the public. They're going to do an autopsy and release her body to us within 48 hours. She wanted to be cremated so we're doing a small family ceremony. Ill keep you updated but it seems my family doesn't want the publicity or her name remembered like that.

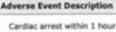

**Stephanie Dawn**
This is a screenshot from a friend

My next door neighbour got the vaccine yesterday. He's dead today. We have been told by relatives that he died of a heart attack. He was in his 70s this cannot be a coincidence.

**Adverse Event Description**

Cardiac arrest within 1 hour Patient had the second vaccine approximately 2 pm on Tuesday Jan 12th He works at the extended care community and was in good health that morning with no complaints. He waited 10-15 minutes at the vaccine admin site and then told them he felt fine and was ready to get back to work. He then was found unresponsive at 3 pm within an hour of the 2nd vaccine. EMS called immediately worked on him 30 minutes in field then 30 minutes at ER was able to put him on life support yet deemed Brain dead 1-14-21 and pronounced dead an hour or so later

ken polanco
@ken27430927

@CBSLA My Story:
My cousin worked at Global community hospital in Santa Ana, he was CT/ex ray tech, on Jan 5th 11:30am he had his 2nd vaccine Pfizer, few hours later he was having a hard time to breathe, that Saturday he passed away. People should know!

9:19 PM · Jan 18, 2021 · Twitter for iPhone

Venting... I had a friend, who is an ER nurse, receive a covid vaccine on December 20th. She proudly rolled up her sleeve and took the shot, complete with pictures posted on FB. I found out today she died at her home on December 26th with "a heart issue". I know for a FACT that she had ZERO underlying issues. I'm sad and very angry all at the same time. WHAT THE $%&@??? You and I know they will NEVER check to see if it was that vaccine that caused it!! Just needed to rant. I don't need negative comments, I just needed to "spew" a bit. TIA.

 52                                 42 Comments

 **Monique Fernandez** ▸ Covid-19 Vaccination Reactions and Feedback
17 hrs · 

I am a wound care nurse working in a facility where the 2nd moderna dose was administered today. I witnessed 4 co workers with stiff arms and pain. I also saw 3 people sit dizzy and confused almost immediately after injection, 1 person was crying with uncontrollable nausea and vomiting. So glad I didn't get the shot. All I'm seeing are negative side effects all around me. 2 department heads left IMMEDIATELY after receiving their vaccine. I'm so tired of all the pro COVID vaxers pushing that we should all get it and that they feel fine.

 **Brand VodkaSoda** @BVodkasoda · 8m
Replying to @abc13houston
Yeah my friends cousin **died** 3 days **after** the mederna vaccine, she **died** yesterday, no underlying conditions, and never had covid #CovidVaccine

♡ 1                    ⟲                    ♡                    ⬆

**♥ 2Cook** @taxgirl13 · 1h

Replying to @HWilson94431347 and @delbigtree

**My** friends brother in law (about age 55) was a doctor in Massachusetts. He received the COVID shot on a Thursday morning and worked the rest of that day. He **died** on Saturday of sepsis. They say it in no way was related to the **vaccine.** Right!!!  Coverup and lies!!!

---

 **Richard Gibson** shared his first post.

· Yesterday at 3:17 PM · ☺

Sadly my mum died at home three and a half hours post Pfizer vaccination. Had shown no adverse symptoms to vaccination prior death. Found unconscious on toilet floor but breathing prior death. Eighty eight years old, frail with underlying medical condition.

😢😮😮 880                                    260 Comments

---

 **Adverse Event Description**

Cardiac arrest within 1 hour Patient had the second vaccine approximately 2 pm on Tuesday Jan 12th He works at the extended care community and was in good health that morning with no complaints. He waited 10-15 minutes at the vaccine admin site and then told them he felt fine and was ready to get back to work. He then was found unresponsive at 3 pm within an hour of the 2nd vaccine. EMS called immediately worked on him 30 minutes in field then 30 minutes at ER was able to put him on life support yet deemed Brain dead 1-14-21 and pronounced dead an hour or so later

 ken polanco
@ken27430927

@CBSLA My Story:
My cousin worked at Global community hospital in Santa Ana, he was CT/ex ray tech, on Jan 5th 11:30am he had his 2nd vaccine Pfizer, few hours later he was having a hard time to breathe, that Saturday he passed away. People should know!

9:19 PM · Jan 18, 2021 · Twitter for iPhone

---

 **Kimberly Carruth Deleanu**

I hope it doesn't take too much longer for everyone else to connect the dots. Sorry about your pa. We have lost two people in our extended family to this mess, an uncle and my sil aunt.

Like · Reply · 7h                                    👍😮 4

**Bump Osteen** @OleNole7 · 4h     ···

My wife's boss, a doctor, was fine after the first shot but got pretty sick after the second. He said "the bones in his head were vibrating."

Health care worker taken to ER just a few hours after getting second COVID-19 **vaccine** shot and later **died**...

**D$** @SolelyConcepts · 52m     ···

A man **died** at **my** mom's nursing home, 20 minutes after taking the COVID **vaccine** so all the staff is scared to take it now. They said that shit cooked. 😂

♡     ⟲ 1     ♡     ⬆

**Write-up:** Patient received vaccine on 1/8/2021. On 1/9/2021 I checked on patient via phone for symptoms or problems and he reported none but mild soreness at injection site. On 1/10/2021 family friend called me to tell me that patient has expired at about 8:00 pm. Patient reportedly complained of "pain" unspecific and collapsed at home. Hospital reportedly told family that it appeared to be a "heart attack".

**#MakeEarthFreeAgain** @Ch1ldk · 2h     ···

**My** 97 year old grandmother took the covid **vaccine** both doses, and is now in the hospital for low blood, and her roommate **died** in her sleep after taking it. Tell me it's "safe" again.

♡     ⟲     ♡ 1     ⬆

# Death on First Exposure

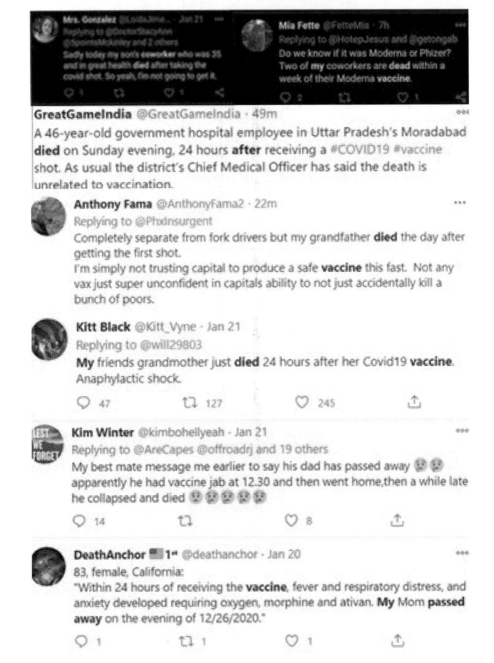

**Mrs. Gonzalez** @LoduJme... · Jan 21
Replying to @DeeterRapkin @SportsMcKinley and 2 others
Sadly today my son's coworker who was 35 and in great health **died** after taking the covid shot. So yeah, I'm not going to get it.

**Mia Fette** @FetteMia · 7h
Replying to @HotepJesus and @getongab
Do we know if it was Moderna or Phizer? Two of **my coworkers** are **dead** within a week of their Moderna **vaccine.**

**GreatGameIndia** @GreatGameIndia · 49m
A 46-year-old government hospital employee in Uttar Pradesh's Moradabad **died** on Sunday evening, 24 hours **after** receiving a #COVID19 #vaccine shot. As usual the district's Chief Medical Officer has said the death is unrelated to vaccination.

**Anthony Fama** @AnthonyFama2 · 22m
Replying to @PhxInsurgent
Completely separate from fork drivers but my grandfather **died** the day after getting the first shot.
I'm simply not trusting capital to produce a safe **vaccine** this fast. Not any vax just super unconfident in capitals ability to not just accidentally kill a bunch of poors.

**Kitt Black** @Kitt_Vyne · Jan 21
Replying to @will29803
**My** friends grandmother just **died** 24 hours after her Covid19 **vaccine.** Anaphylactic shock.

♡ 47    ⟲ 127    ♡ 245    ⬆

**Kim Winter** @kimbohellyeah · Jan 21
Replying to @AreCapes @offroadrj and 19 others
My best mate message me earlier to say his dad has passed away 😲😲 apparently he had vaccine jab at 12.30 and then went home,then a while late he collapsed and died 😲😲😲😲😲

♡ 14    ⟲    ♡ 8    ⬆

**DeathAnchor** 🏴1ᵃ @deathanchor · Jan 20
83, female, California:
"Within 24 hours of receiving the **vaccine**, fever and respiratory distress, and anxiety developed requiring oxygen, morphine and ativan. **My Mom passed away** on the evening of 12/26/2020."

♡ 1    ⟲ 1    ♡ 1    ⬆

# Additional Evidence and Special Concerns

# Vaccine Impact on Fertility

**XI.** Several vaccine candidates are expected to induce the formation of humoral antibodies against spike proteins of SARS-CoV-2. Syncytin-1 (see Gallaher, B., "Response to nCoV2019 Against Backdrop of Endogenous Retroviruses" - http://virological.org/t/response-to-ncov2019-against-backdrop-of-endogenous-retroviruses/396), which is derived from human endogenous retroviruses (HERV) and is responsible for the development of a placenta in mammals and humans and is therefore an essential prerequisite for a successful pregnancy, is also found in homologous form in the spike proteins of SARS viruses. There is no indication whether antibodies against spike proteins of SARS viruses would also act like anti-Syncytin-1 antibodies. However, if this were to be the case this would then also prevent the formation of a placenta which would result in vaccinated women essentially becoming infertile. To my knowledge, Pfizer/BioNTech has yet to release any samples of written materials provided to patients, so it is unclear what, if any, information regarding (potential) fertility-specific risks caused by antibodies is included.

According to section 10.4.2 of the Pfizer/BioNTech trial protocol, a woman of childbearing potential (WOCBP) is eligible to participate if she is not pregnant or breastfeeding, and is using an acceptable contraceptive method as described in the trial protocol during the intervention period (for a minimum of 28 days after the last dose of study intervention).

This means that it could take a relatively long time before a noticeable number of cases of post-

80

# Vaccine Impact on Menstruation

## Menstural symptoms after Moderna vaccine

`Moderna`

Two of my roommates received their first dose of moderna on Sunday. One has an IUD and the other is on standard hormonal birth control, and both are having abnormal menstural symptoms. The one with the IUD has not had bleeding or spotting in a year, and yesterday had to go to the ER because she started heavy bleeding. The ER doctors believed it was a stress response to the vaccine. The other began her period today even though she had it just a week ago. Has anyone else had abnormal menstural symptoms?

> **Kenziry** 🖊 6 days ago
>
> I generally don't have cramps anymore having an IUD. But since I've been bleeding so heavily the past few days I've been cramping and they're fairly strong.

> Embarrassed-Half-994 6 hours ago
>
> Yes! I'm seeing more posts like this too. I am having the worst PMS of my life. I typically have a very regular cycle/symptoms.
>
> ⬆ 1 ⬇  🗨 Reply  Give Award  Share  Report  Save

> amacdc 4 days ago
>
> I have periods like clockwork, arriving on my cycle-predicted day without fail. I got vaccinated 2 days ago and started my period this morning, EIGHT days early. I'm relieved I'm not the only one!

> ratcats 15 days ago
>
> Mine was a week late and I'm never late.
>
> ⬆ 2 ⬇  🗨 Reply  Give Award  Share  Report  Save

> **cootercanoe42** 🖊 15 days ago
>
> Mine too! So interesting.
>
> ⬆ 1 ⬇  🗨 Reply  Give Award  Share  Report  Save

# Lost Pregnancy, Spontaneous Abortion

starting to feel lethargic and weak. Had menses with increased blessed. Called physician to have blood work done to see if I was experiencing anemia. Blood work complete on 12/31/2020. On 1/3/2021, I woke up with blood blisters all over the inside of my mouth and petechia on my trunk and bilateral upper and lower extremities. I called my primary physician to report the symptoms. He suggested to go to the ER if my symptoms worsened. Later that evening I started with a nose bleed and did go to the ER. Upon arrival to the ER, my platelet count was 9. I was admitted to the hospital and diagnosed with ITP.

My doctor told me "Do NOT get the Covid-19 vaccine!" 😡 she said she's had several pregnant patients have miscarriages after receiving it, even though she did not recommend the experimental vaccine to them.

I now know of two pregnant ladies who got these poison injections "to protect their babies" both have miscarried after the first dose. This madness needs to end NOW! People just STOP believing this is for your safety and STOP believing the contrived lengths the media is going to in order to make you believe this is all in the name of public safety and betterment!! If it weren't for the media and this planned pandemic, this poison and ridiculous social distancing, masking, etc wouldn't exist either!!

3h   Like   Reply

 **Diane Wheat-Stephenson**
My friends sister was so excited to be 34 weeks and to be "allowed" to get her Covid vaccine to protect her and her baby. Her baby passed away pre-birth 48 hours later.
They are still waiting on autopsy results.

 **Cheese Tortle** @hereforthemad · 4h
Replying to @pancakeliberty
I'm so sorry, infuriating. May I ask how old? I don't mean to be insensitive but **my** curiosity gets the best of me. I just saw a 35 year old pregnant mother got **vaccinated** and the healthy 28 week year old baby **died**.

 1               4

 **Alex Berenson** ✓ @AlexBerenson · 19h
A scientist at a biotechnology company thinks the **vaccines** may increase **miscarriage** risk by stimulating interferon production.

Make sure to read the last screenshot about potential long-term autoimmune effects, too. "At this point only time will tell." Great!

# Case Descriptions Below From VAERS Database

**As of 2/12/2021 VAERS data search included 34 cases where Vaccine is COVID19 and Symptom is LOST PREGNANCY**

**Found 34 cases where Vaccine is COVID19 and Symptom is Aborted pregnancy or Abortion or Abortion spontaneous** or Abortion spontaneous complete or Abortion spontaneous incomplete or Abortion threatened or Foetal-maternal haemorrhage or Foetal cardiac disorder or Foetal damage or Foetal death or Foetal disorder or Foetal distress syndrome or Foetal heart rate abnormal or Foetal heart rate deceleration or Foetal heart rate deceleration abnormality or Foetal heart rate decreased or Foetal heart rate disorder or Foetal heart rate increased or Foetal hypokinesia or Foetal malformation or Foetal malpresentation or Foetal monitoring abnormal or Foetal movement disorder or Foetal movements decreased or Foetal non-stress test abnormal or Placental disorder or Pregnancy induced hypertension or Premature baby or Premature baby death or Premature delivery or Premature labour or Premature rupture of membranes or Premature separation of placenta or Stillbirth or Ultrasound foetal abnormal

**VAERS ID: 932107**
Age: 37.0 Sex: Female Location: New York Vaccinated: 2021-01-06
Onset: 2021-01-08 **Days after vaccination: 2**
COVID19: COVID19 PFIZER/BIONTECH
SMQs:, Dystonia (broad), Pregnancy, labor and delivery complications and risk factors (excl abortions and stillbirth) (narrow), **Termination of pregnancy** and risk of abortion (narrow)
**Birth Defect? Yes**
Write-up: Pfizer-BioNTech COVID-19 Vaccine EUA Miscarriage - (date of vaccination 1/6/21, miscarriage symptoms (cramping) started 1/8/21, confirmed 1/10/21; estimated date of delivery 8/30/21

**VAERS ID: 1028819**
Age: 39.0  Sex: Female   Location: Missouri   Vaccinated: 2020-12-18
Onset:   2021-02-03     **Days after vaccination:  47**
COVID19: COVID19 PFIZER/BIONTECH
**Birth Defect? Yes**
Diagnostic Lab Data: 2/3 - **ultrasound showed no heartbeat** 2/5 - beta hcg quant -
41,xxx 2/7 - beta hcg quant - 40,xxx 2/11 - 2nd confirmation ultrasound. 2/11 - beta
hcg quant - 35,xxx
Write-up: **First trimester miscarriage after receiving both vaccine doses while
pregnant.** Due date 9/17/2021

**VAERS ID: 1025363**
Age: 40.0  Sex: Female     Location: Ohio    Vaccinated: 2021-02-05
Onset:   2021-02-06     **Days after vaccination:  1**
COVID19: COVID19 PFIZER/BIONTECH
SMQs:, **Anaphylactic reaction** (broad)
Symptoms: **Abortion spontaneous**, Foetal heart rate abnormal, Headache, Nausea,
Pyrexia, Rash, Rash erythematous, Ultrasound uterus abnormal, Vomiting
Diagnostic Lab Data: Pregnancy was on 2/11, Second vaccine dose was on 2/5
Write-up: About 12 hours after the vaccine I developed headache, fever 100.5, nausea
and vomiting, and red rash across my chest up to my neck and under both breasts. All
symptoms but the rash improved the following day. I went to have my 8 week
pregnancy US **6 days after this second vaccine dose and there was no fetal heart
rate.** The baby measured 8.7mm and there should be a heart rate when the baby
measures $g7mm. I had all of my pregnancy symptoms up through the day of the
vaccine and then they disappeared the day my vaccine symptoms improved. I do not
have a history of miscarriage.

| VAERS ID: | 1006169 (history) |
|---|---|
| Form: | Version 2.0 |
| Age: | 43.0 |
| Sex: | Female |
| Location: | Massachusetts |

| Vaccinated: | 2021-01-14 |
|---|---|
| Onset: | 2021-01-18 |
| Days after vaccination: | 4 |
| Submitted: | 0000-00-00 |
| Entered: | 2021-02-05 |

| Vaccination / Manufacturer | Lot / Dose | Site / Route |
|---|---|---|
| **COVID19**: COVID19 (COVID19 (PFIZER-BIONTECH)) / PFIZER/BIONTECH | - / 2 | RA / IM |

**Symptoms:**

Abdominal pain, Abortion spontaneous, COVID-19, Exposure during pregnancy, Full blood count, Haemorrhage, Human chorionic gonadotropin positive, Pregnancy, Pregnancy test positive, Surgery, Transfusion, Ultrasound abdomen abnormal, Ultrasound scan vagina

I was approximately 4 weeks pregnant at the time that I received dose #1 (12/23/20)- I was unaware of the pregnancy. I was diagnosed with COVID on 12/28/20, but was first symptomatic on 12/24. I attributed my s/s initially to the vaccine. I was eventually tested on 12/28/20, as my symptoms worsened and I was positive for COVID. On 1/14/21 I received my second dose, my COVID s/s had been resolved since 1/4/21. On the evening of 1/18/21 I started experiencing mild abdominal pain. This progressed, on the evening 1/20 the pain was no longer tolerable. I went to the ER where I hemorrhaged and needed emergency surgery and a blood transfusion for a miscarriage. The surgery ultimately took place in the early morning hours of 1/22/21, followed by the blood transfusion.

**VAERS ID: 1033516**

Age: 32.0  Sex: Female    Location: Minnesota    Vaccinated: 2021-01-29
Onset:  2021-02-15    **Days after vaccination: 17**
COVID19: COVID19 MODERNA
Symptoms: **Abortion spontaneous, Exposure during pregnancy,** Headache, Pain in extremity, Sleep disorder, Ultrasound abdomen abnormal, Ultrasound scan vagina abnormal
**Birth Defect? Yes**
Preexisting Conditions: No chronic health issues, otherwise very healthy.
Diagnostic Lab Data: On 2/16/21 I had an abdominal and vaginal ultrasounds, which confirmed absence of fetus in the uterus. Eptopic pregnancy was ruled out. MD was consulted on the same day regarding miscarriage.
Write-up: **At the time of administration of the first does of Moderna vaccine, I was 6 weeks pregnant. I had confirmed pregnancy** with home positive test and missed period. I had an estimated due date of 9/24/2021. This was my 4th pregnancy. I have had two uncomplicated pregnancies to term. In September 2020 experienced a chemical pregnancy with early pregnancy loss at 5 weeks. After 24 hours I felt "normal". 2 weeks and 3 days following the first dose of Moderna, I had a miscarriage. On the night of 2/15/21 **I lost the pregnancy with vaginal bleeding**, bright red blood, passing tissue, clots/ sac. I had an **uneventful pregnancy up to that point**, feeling well as I had with prior pregnancies.

---

**VAERS ID: 990450**

Age: 33.0  Sex: Female    Location: Indiana    Vaccinated:    2021-01-11
Onset:  2021-01-16    **Days after vaccination: 5**
COVID19: COVID19 PFIZER/BIONTECH
Symptoms: **Abortion spontaneous,** Congenital anomaly, Exposure during pregnancy, SARS-CoV-2 test negative
Write-up: **Miscarriage after 2nd vaccine**; This is a spontaneous report from a contactable nurse reported for herself. This 33-year-old female patient The patient had no known allergies. The patient had no other vaccine in four weeks, no other medications in two weeks. **The patient was pregnant.** Last menstrual date was 14Dec2020. Delivery due date was 16Sep2021. Gestation period was 3 weeks. The **patient experienced miscarriage on 16 Jan2021 after 2nd vaccine.** AE resulted in congenital anomaly or birth defect. The patient had COVID tested/nasal swab post vaccination with negative results
Sender"s Comments: Based on the available information, **a causal relationship between event miscarriage after the second COVID-19 vaccination and BNT162B2**
**(PFIZER-BIONTECH COVID-19 VACCINE) cannot be completely excluded.**

**VAERS ID: 995949**
Age: 39.0  Sex: Female    Location: Wisconsin      Vaccinated:       2021-01-22
Onset:  2021-02-01      **Days after vaccination:  10**
COVID19: COVID19 PFIZER/BIONTECH
**Birth Defect? Yes**
Symptoms: **Abortion spontaneous**
Write-up: **Miscarriage reported**

---

**VAERS ID: 1006169**
Age: 43.0  Sex: Female    Location: Massachusetts  Vaccinated: 2021-01-14
Onset:  2021-01-18      **Days after vaccination:  4**
COVID19: COVID19 PFIZER/BIONTECH
Write-up: I was approximately 4 weeks pregnant at the time that I received dose #1
(12/23/20)- I was unaware of the pregnancy. I was diagnosed with COVID on
12/28/20, but was first symptomatic on 12/24. I attributed my s/s initially to the
vaccine. I was eventually tested on 12/28/20, as my symptoms worsened and I was
positive for COVID. On 1/14/21 I received my second dose, my COVID s/s had been
resolved since 1/4/21. On the evening of 1/18/21 I started experiencing mild abdominal
pain. This progressed, on the evening 1/20 the pain was no longer tolerable. I went to
the ER where I **hemorrhaged and needed emergency surgery and a blood
transfusion for a miscarriage.** The surgery ultimately took place in the early morning
hours of 1/22/21, followed by the blood transfusion.

---

**VAERS ID: 1023866**
Age: 28.0  Sex: Female    Location: North Carolina  Vaccinated: 2021-01-15
Onset:  2021-02-11      **Days after vaccination:  27**
COVID19: COVID19 PFIZER/BIONTECH
Symptoms: **Abortion spontaneous**, Exposure during pregnancy, Full blood count,
Gynaecological examination abnormal, Human chorionic gonadotropin decreased,
Vaginal haemorrhage
Write-up: **Miscarriage at 6 weeks 1 day. Vaginal bleeding and decline in HCG
hormone. Pregnancy not viable.**

---

**VAERS ID: 1028368**
Age: 32.0  Sex: Female    Location: California      Vaccinated: 2021-01-27
Onset:  2021-02-05      Days after vaccination:  9
Symptoms: **Abortion spontaneous**, Exposure during pregnancy
Write-up: **Miscarriage in first trimester.** First dose received 12/22/2020 Conception
date 01/03/2021 Second dose 01/27/2021 Miscarriage started 02/03/2021 First
pregnancy. No other medical problems or pregnancy risks.

# Breast Feeding Risks After Vaccination

## Case Descriptions Below From VAERS Database

**VAERS ID: 931851**
**Maternal exposure during breast feeding**
Write-up: I am currently breastfeeding my 5-month-old son. I received my first vaccine on 12/28/2020 and directly **breastfed within 4 hours of receiving the vaccine.** Two days after my vaccine my son was at daycare and had two large diarrhea blowouts and two large emeses followed by a 1-minute episode **where he was limp with entire body cyanosis and in-and-out of consciousness.** He also had a maculopapular **rash on his torso.** EMS was called.

**VAERS ID: 917888**
**Maternal exposure during breast feeding**
Write-up: I am breastfeeding **my 15 month old son and he got a rash on his abdomen and face that has progressed more over past several days.** He has had no fever but acts like he doesn't feel great as he was not eating like his normal self. I don't know if the rash is related or not but it is **during the time of the vaccine.**

**VAERS ID: 930348**
**Maternal exposure during breast feeding**
Write-up: I am breastfeeding. **My daughter had seizure like episodes** starting on Saturday 1/2, Sunday 1/3, Monday, 1/4 and 2 times on Tuesday 1/5.

**VAERS ID: 905801**
**Maternal exposure during breast feeding**
Write-up: I am breastfeeding **my 20 month old and she developed a rash on trunk.** Maculopapular.

**VAERS ID: 903355**
**Maternal exposure during breast feeding**
Write-up: **Breastfeeding toddler developed rash to torso, back, and cheek**

# Healthcare Worker Comments, Observations, Occupational Pressures

in Directors Of Nursing
14m · ⊠

m having a moral dilemma and could use some
dvice. We had our Covid vaccination clinic
esterday. A resident that received the vaccine
oded and died within 12 hours. While it is
robably coincidental I still feel this should be
eported to VAERS. I am being directed not to
eport by corporate. I am leaning to report
egardless. What would you do? I had already put

Was my post deleted? I posted
saying my Dad's girlfriend and
her colleague both reacted to
the vaccine last week. Her
colleague collapsed during
surgery in an operating
theatre. Nhs workers.

Khwezi Shange @khwezi_sh... · Jan 7 ···
Replying to @Tman_once @somgabi and 2
others
Well this last one is tragic,
A 41 yr old "healthy" medical worker.
One of 538 people who got the **vaccine** and
**passed away.**
This one is the noteworthy one to me.
There must be thousands who've taken
**vaccines** by now.
And her without previous illnesses died.

 5:13 ◍ ▦

 ← 🔵 Covid-19 Vaccinati... Q ···

Ok let's just get down to the details, this
vaccine is unsafe I work in long term care
we vaccinated all of our residents! They
almost all had a temperature at some
point one had obvious neurological
responses and another I had to send to
ER with p 174 r 25, she appeared fine and
if I didn't take her vitals when I did I
guarantee you she would have died! They
gave her tons of meds to get her back to
normal...point is this vaccine isn't safe if
that was my experience with 12 residents
in my care that means 1/12 could have
died, 1/12 could possibly have
permanent neurological issues, and
12/12 had minor temporary reactions
and that is all one day after the first shot,
then the Er doc proceeds to tell the
daughter he isn't sure if it was from the
vaccine...1f he mean she had no history of
heart problems ever...I told the daughter
everyone has to make their own choices
on this stuff and I suggested she do her
own research before she decides to take
second dose lol wtf that's what kills me
we just keep insisting people take it and
nothing is a possibly a good reason to not
take it

 dess 🦴 @desstdabest · 4m                    ···
**My** coworker told me two people she knows took the **vaccine**... one **died** &
the other is paralyzed...

90

**Heidi Neckelmann**
January 5 at 9:00 PM · 🌐

The love of my life, my husband Gregory Michael MD
an Obstetrician that had his office in Mount Sinai Medical Center in
Miami Beach Died the day before yesterday due to a strong reaction
to the COVID vaccine.
He was a very healthy 56 year old, loved by everyone in the
community delivered hundreds of healthy babies and worked tireless
through the pandemic.
He was vaccinated with the Pfizer vaccine at MSMC on December 18, 3
days later he saw a strong set of petechiae on his feet and hands
which made him seek attention at the emergency room at MSMC. The
CBC that was done at his arrival showed his platelet count to be 0 (A
normal platelet count ranges from 150,000 to 450,000 platelets per
microliter of blood.) he was admitted in the ICU with a diagnosis of
acute ITP caused by a reaction to the COVID vaccine. A team of expert
doctors tried for 2 weeks to raise his platelet count to no avail. Experts
from all over the country were involved in his care. No matter what
they did, the platelets count refused to go up. He was conscious and
energetic through the whole process but 2 days before a last resort
surgery,  he got a hemorrhagic stroke caused by the lack of platelets
that took his life in a matter of minutes.
He was a pro vaccine advocate that is why he got it himself.
I believe that people should be aware that side effects can happened,
that it is not good for everyone and in this case destroyed a beautiful
life, a perfect family, and has affected so many people in the
community
Do not let his death be in vain please save more lives by making this
information news.

**DaveX** @buzzconstruct · 5h
Replying to @VictorMeldrew69 and @Lesqueenb
**My** gran had a stoke 2 hours after pfizer **vaccine** Tuesday she **died**. **My** wife
works in a care home same happening there having stokes after the **vaccine**.
Classed as a stroke death though

**WhatIsLife** @WhatIsL03139271 · 13h
Replying to @NotAnAndroidv2
**My** mom's friend works in a care home where 8 people have **died** in the last
week. All since **vaccine**.

♡          ⊏⊐          ♡ 1          ⬆

**Peter Gordon** ▸ **Covid-19 Vaccination Feedback**
7 hrs · 🌐

A 58 year old nurse I've know for 15 years died today, I found her in her room in bed, she was pretty healthy, she was semi retired............She received the vaccine a week and a half ago, I'll be doing some serious investigation, as I don't believe it was her time today. gutted is not the word.

 803                                                        203 Comments

 ♥ **2Cook** @taxgirl13 · 1h                                      •••
Replying to @HWilson94431347 and @delbigtree

**My** friends brother in law (about age 55) was a doctor in Massachusetts. He received the COVID shot on a Thursday morning and worked the rest of that day. He **died** on Saturday of sepsis. They say it in no way was related to the **vaccine**. Right!!! Coverup and lies!!!

♡           ⟲            ♡           ⤒

# Detailed Personal Accounts

**Shoshana Kiki**
January 10 at 11:05 AM · 🌐

Reactions to the Pfizer vaccines in the European
Union until 8th of January. And not all reactions
have been reported. Deaths are being labelled as
'Investigations'.

👍😮😢 56                                          23 Comments

**Chris Cowell** @ChrisCowell37 · 8m    ···
Feel so much worse after the **vaccine** than I
did when I had covid. Never had a headache
like this 😫 literally hurts to keep my head
up.

**Tim Davis** ▸ Covid-19 Vaccination Feedback    ···
10 mins · 🌐

My Dad is 82 and had the Pfizer vac on 30th Dec.
He reported feeling really unwell two days later.
By the 4th day they were really worried about him
As he was having breathing problems, then vomitted.
He was rushed to hospital straight after this, meanwhile a few of them in the home where he lives
were pcr tested for Covid.
My sister and I went to see him in A and E they said he may not make it through the night that
was 3 days ago. He had nuemonia and was gravely ill.
Meanwhile his covid test came back positive afyer the vaccine.
11 days after taking the V he is still fighting for his life.
3 other residents from his care home went to hospital and passed away that same day.
Whilst my dad wasnt in the healthiest of conditions, he was still chipper in convasations we had
on boxing day and on 27th dec.
We cant say for sure that this is any reaction to the vaccine, and as his illness is being blamed on
covid. My gut feeling is that the vaccine has everything to do with him being so close to death,
but I have no evidence so cannot say it for sure.
He is on oxygen at present and comfortanle.we have been told.
I would not go near it with a pole personally. It was too quick to be released and when you
research it you find that PEG carriers can have adverse effects let alone the RNA instructions
themselves. I have read the reports on how previous coronvirus's vaccines bever worked and did
advise my dad accordingly. He was reticent at first but then was advised it would.be best for him.
These vaccines should be halted until we know a whole lot more about them.
Regards
Timo

😢😮👍 36                                          15 Comments

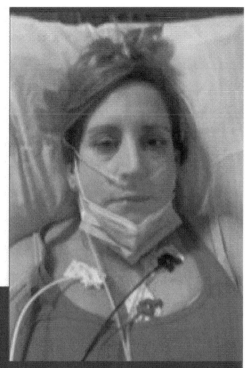

**Stacee Dominguez Hanson**
18 hrs · 🌐

My Pfizer Covid vaccine story....

I have waited to post my story out of fear of negative comments, therefore I'm asking you to please don't leave a negative comment because this is MY story. Thanks

I was excited to be chosen to receive the Pfizer Covid 19 vaccine. I have been a nurse for 20 years and love what I do for my community. I felt that everyone in my life, including my patients, family as well as myself would benefit if i receive the vaccine. After all what could be so bad about a vaccine? I believe vaccines are good. I'm healthy, No health conditions and No allergies.

On 12/18/20 around 12:30 pm, I go to the designated station pull up my right sleeve and receive the injection. I think, "okay, that wasn't so bad" and I leave to go to the waiting area for 15 minutes to make sure no reactions occur.

As I was in the elevator going down, one floor, to the seating area, I felt some dizziness. I think to myself that I just stepped wrong in the elevator. I get to the floor and was greeted from a nurse that asked me to wait for a minute to be seated. I then felt a big wave of dizziness over my body. I asked if I could sit now as I was feeling really dizzy and my legs feel like noodles. The nurse kindly said yes, sit anywhere you'd like. I sat down and she asked how I was feeling? I said kinda dizzy and weird but I don't think it's anything. A sweet girl sitting across from me said to me, "it's not in your head, I feel the same thing." We looked at each other with a bewildered look in our eyes. Then the girl sitting across from me said that she was starting to feel a tickle in her throat. A few minutes later, I started feeling the same, a tickle in my throat. We both agreed that it still probably wasn't anything and maybe we needed to drink some water. Next she said to the nurse that she is feeling "fullness" in her throat. The medical personnel quickly took her away to one of two back rooms to possibly start an IV. I sat there alone when I also started feeling a "fullness" in my throat and I looked around but didn't see anyone. Then the Physician came up to me and asked me how I was feeling? I told her, "I feel fullness in my throat also," with deer in a headlight look on my face. She took me to the other room in the back, just in case we need to start an IV. An IV? For what? I was confused and thought I'm okay just feeling a little strange.

I go to the back room and blood pressure showed 187/100 and pulse 120. I was asked by all personnel if I had HTN, allergies or allergies to the flu vaccine. I said No I don't have any allergie or HTN. The fullness in my throat quickly escalated to feeling like I was being choked with extreme heat inside my body that started at my throat and waved down to my abdomen and back up. That's when I got an IV, Benadryl, solumedrol and my first injection of epinephrine. Now my blood pressure and heart rate was even higher and I start shaking uncontrollably due to the epi. I stare at the ceiling and I feel this is surreal and not me, I still don't quite realize what's happening until the medical person standing on my left side asks the physician on my right, she's having an anaphylactic reaction, isn't she? The physician on

I was saved by not only great health care personnel and medicine, but but the grace of God also. Thank you God for saving my life!

Thank you for listening to my story. Please be careful if you receive the Pfizer Covid vaccine and feel free to share my story... thank you to my friends and family that helped me recuperate, I couldn't have done it without you. Love you all and feel so greatly that you are in my life. 🙏
♥ 🙏

My sister-in-law lost her father two weeks ago. He was diagnosed with Covid as the cause of death. He was 90 years old but lived independently in his own house. He walked to get his vaccine just a couple of days before he collapsed. His legs just went from under him. He died in hospital just four days after his collapse. He was being treated for memory issues before but no other medical issues. He was considered physically fit and well for his age. I don't know which vaccine he had - it was either AZ or Pfizer.

Just a question how does a death after a positive test result within 28 days equal Covid death diagnosis (however you died) and death after a vaccine administered six days before not vaccine related? Can someone explain the scientific logic here?

**BLINDNESS - From the 2/18/2021 release of VAERS data:**
Found <u>9 cases</u> where Vaccine targets COVID-19 (COVID19) and Manufacturer is PFIZER/BIONTECH and Symptom is Blindness

## Case Description Below From VAERS Database

**Write-up:** central retinal vein occlusion resulting in **loss of sight to right eye** I was on computer and **had bright flashes of lights the lost vision in the eye about 2 1/2 hours after receiving vaccine.** CRVO is rare in my age with no health problems. Saw ER doctor that night then ophthalmologist the next morning who diagnosed me. **I am currently prescribed a baby aspirin and will have to get injections in my eye** when macular edema occurs, an expected occurrence with a blood clot in the retinal vein

# Additional Information on Adverse Events

VAERS REPORT AS OF THE 28th:

The latest data from the Department of Health and Human Services (HHS) shows there have now been 40,433 adverse events from the Covid-19 vaccinations in the USA.

This includes 127 deaths, along with 769 cases of abdominal pain, along with 1,410 cases of amnesia, dizziness, disorientation, vertigo, confusion and dilirium, along with 1,531 cases of fatigue, along with 1,117 cases of herpes, along with 769 cases of abdominal pain, along with 717 cases of headache and head injury from falls, along with 521 cases of influenza-like-illness, along with 57 cases of blindness and deafness, along with 175 cases of eye swelling, eye discharge and eye pain, along with tens of thousands of other ill effects."

National Vaccine
Information Center
Your Health, Your Family, Your Choice

MedAlerts Home

Search Results

From the 2/4/2021 release of VAERS data:

Found 468 cases where Vaccine is COVID19 and Life Threatening

Case Details

This is page 2 out of 47

# Unexpected String of Allergic Reactions Causes Delays at 'Vaccination Super Station' Near Petco Park

Allergic reactions in some Moderna vaccine recipients caused delays Wednesday at San Diego County's new "Vaccination Super Station" near downtown's Petco Park, County health officials confirmed.

| VAERS ID | Vaccine Type | Adverse Event Description |
|---|---|---|
| 909095-1 | COVID19 VACCINE (COVID19) | on 12/24/2020 the resident was sleepy and stayed in bed most of the shift. He stated he was doing okay but requested pain medication for his legs at 250PM. At 255AM on 12/25/2020 the resident was observed in bed lying still, pale, eyes half open and foam coming from mouth and unresponsive. He was not breathing and with no pulse |
| 910363-1 | COVID19 VACCINE (COVID19) | Patient had mild hypotension, decreased oral intake, somnolence starting 3 days after vaccination and death 5 days after administration. He did have advanced dementia and was hospice eligible based on history of aspiration pneumonia. |
| 912143-1 | COVID19 VACCINE (COVID19) | Vaccine administered with no immediate adverse reaction at 11:29am. Vaccine screening questions were completed and resident was not feeling sick and temperature was 98F. At approximately 1:30pm the resident passed away. |
| 912733-1 | COVID19 VACCINE (COVID19) | My grandmother died a few hours after receiving the moderna covid vaccine booster 1. While I don?t expect that the events are related, the treating hospital did not acknowledge this and I wanted to be sure a report was made. |
| 914621-1 | COVID19 VACCINE (COVID19) | Resident in our long term care facility who received first dose of Moderna COVID-19 Vaccine on 12/22/2020, only documented side effect was mild fatigue after receiving. She passed away on 12/27/2020 of natural causes per report. Has previously been in & out of hospice care, resided in nursing home for 9+ years, elderly with dementia. Due to proximity of vaccination we felt we should report the death, even though it is not believed to be related. |
| 914690-1 | COVID19 VACCINE (COVID19) | Within 24 hours of receiving the vaccine, fever and respiratory distress, and anxiety developed requiring oxygen, morphine and ativan. My Mom passed away on the evening of 12/26/2020. |
| 914805-1 | COVID19 VACCINE (COVID19) | RESIDENT CODED AND EXPIRED |
| 914895-1 | COVID19 VACCINE (COVID19) | Injection given on 12/28/20 - no adverse events and no issues yesterday; Death today, 12/30/20, approx.. 2am today (unknown if related - Administrator marked as natural causes) |
| 914917-1 | COVID19 VACCINE (COVID19) | Death by massive heart attack. Pfizer-BioNTech COVID-19 Vaccine EUA |
| 914961-1 | COVID19 VACCINE (COVID19) | pt passed away with an hour to hour and 1/2 of receiving vaccine. per nursing home staff they did not expect pt to make it many more days. pt was unresponsive in room when shot was given. per nursing home staff pt was 14 + days post covid |
| 914994-1 | COVID19 VACCINE (COVID19) | pt was a nursing home pt. pt received first dose of covid vaccine. pt was monitored for 15 minutes after getting shot. staff reported that pt was 15 days post covid. Pt passed away with in 90 minutes of getting vaccine |

# Compromised Healthcare Workers And 'Vaccine Sickness'

There is another very serious situation right now that hardly anyone is talking about and that is physically compromised healthcare workers.

Because many of them are being pressured into getting covid vaccinations to continue in their positions, doctors, nurses, and other care providers, many such workers may be attempting to do their jobs while experiencing first, second, and even third-degree anaphylactic reactions and covering those effects up or ignoring them in order to continue.

Such workers are worse than drunk drivers on the road. Any of them can make a potentially lethal error in the performance of their duties and this possibility cannot be ignored. Of paramount concern here are instances of what they are describing as **"Brain Fog"**.

Difficulty with memory and attention are serious disabilities that will most certainly compromise their ability to administer medications and conduct many common medical procedures with a proper degree of competence. Now that you have read some of the VAERS reports and first-hand complaints made by CV-19 vaccine recipients you have to wonder just how good some healthcare workers are going to be performing their duties.

Healthcare workers attempting to work in a daze will undoubtedly be subject to a mental condition that will be the cause of all kinds of serious errors in patient care and if one of them is treating you, you may never know if your provider should be in a hospital bed themselves, because they probably wont tell anyone, either because their employers are demanding that they cover shifts, or simply because they need their paychecks.

Personal comments posted on social media by some such workers follow. Given what they describe, the extent of the problem and what other examples of procedural lapses exist are things we can only guess at. Clearly even simple procedures like administering CV-19 vaccines are multiplying. VAERS is rife with examples of incorrect dosage examples as you will see.

After reading several accounts thus far in my research for this book, of previously vaccinated surgeons collapsing in an operating theater in the middle of a procedure, such possibilities are far from reassuring.

blackbird24601 12 days ago

I got mine a week ago- Saturday at 1030.

Felt like hell til Tuesday. Today I was at work realizing I could not smell or taste.

Got swabbed- will know results Sunday.

Was kept at work REGARDLESS.

I am praying this was a SE. I basically isolate cos I am a nurse working with cancer patients.

I'm feeling so sad- kissed hubby a lot (as we are wont to do) And hugged my son last night.

Anyone else have loss of taste/smell???

 r/CovidVaccinated · Posted by u/prnorm 1 day ago

## Anybody experience "brain fog" as a side effect of the vaccine (specifically Pfizer)?

Hi all. My wife had the first dose of the Pfizer vaccine just over 24 hours ago. Earlier today (about 18 hours after the injection) she started feeling what she described as disconnected, slow, and forgetful. She can't really hold a thought or conversation and loses her train of thought easily. She just wants to sit and do nothing. She is a mental health counselor and had to cancel her sessions today because she couldn't focus at all. I think it sounds similar to what people describe as the brain fog with covid.

It's only been about a half a day now, but I'm just wondering if it would make sense that this could be a side-effect of the vaccine? I hear it talked about as a side-effect of Covid itself, so does that mean it could also be a side effect of the the vaccine? Anybody else experience this?

 Antoni Serra-Torres 🍎 @DrAntoniSerraT1 · Jan 26
Brain **fog** is one of the most reported secondary effect of mRNA **vaccine** among colleagues so far.

 r/CovidVaccinated · Posted by u/MemeLordBeefCakes 10 days ago

## Took the vaccine yesterday at 2pm. Noticed a very odd thing.

spoiler

I took the covid vaccine today at 2pm and about 30-40 minutes after I felt very dizzy, I was at a McDonalds trying to order a Mc Double (unhealthy choice I know) but I couldn't seem to remember what I was doing. I couldn't even formulate words properly and I forgot what I was doing entirely. The feeling of cloudy thoughts went away fairly quick maybe two minutes tops. Yet still it's unsettling and I'm afraid of what it's going to be like tomorrow. Have been noticing extreme muscle/body pain, over heating, dizziness, and chills. It's 2:43 am now and I cannot sleep but I hope this is all just how it should be and nothing is wrong.

**Jas**
@Jvzxo

So my job offered us the covid vaccine about 2 weeks ago , and now my coworker who is high risk for covid has been bugging .. the vaccine is supposed to give you symptoms but sis is forgetting shit we talked about just last week. Coughing like crazy etc.

| 907710-1 | PFIZER\BIONTECH | 40-49 years | About 30 minutes after injection felt brain fog and had a hard time finding words; About 30 minutes after injection felt brain fog and had a hard time finding words; It's like we were having to concentrate more than usual to do routine stuff; This is a spontaneous report from a contactable consumer (patient himself). A 44-year-old male received BNT162B2 (PFIZER-BIONTECH COVID-19 VACCINE, Lot number EJ1685), intramuscular on the left arm, as first single dose on 20Dec2020 (at 06:30) for COVID-19 immunisation. The patient did not have a relevant medical history. No relevant concomitant medications were provided. About 30 minutes after injection felt brain fog and had a hard time finding words. Another nurse that got vaccinated at the same time felt the same way. It's like we were having to concentrate more than usual to do routine stuff. The patient was not treated for the events. The patient did not perform COVID test before vaccination but after vaccination Nasal Swab, Rapid PCR, was Negative. He was recovering from the events.; Sender's Comments: Linked Report(s) : US-PFIZER INC-2020504556 same drug, same event and different patient |

**From the 2/18/2021 release of VAERS data:**
*Found 31 cases where Vaccine targets COVID-19 (COVID19) and Manufacturer is PFIZER/BIONTECH and Symptom is Incorrect dosage administered or Incorrect dose administered or Incorrect drug administration duration or Incorrect drug dosage form administered or Incorrect product storage or Incorrect route of product administration or Incorrect storage of drug or Product preparation error or Product preparation issue*

# Serious Vaccine Administration Errors

## Case Descriptions Below From VAERS Database

---

**VAERS ID:**     913893
**Incorrect dose administered**
Write-up: **Nurse did not add normal saline diluent to vial; drew up and administered concentrated vaccine of 0.3ml the equivalent of 5 concentrated doses/ it sounds like I got 30 times the regular dose.**

---

**VAERS ID:**     994023
**Product preparation error**
Write-up: **Patient received immunization from vial containing diluents in the amount of 1.0 rather than 1.8 ml 0.9% sodium chloride,** so dose was concentrated.

---

**VAERS ID:**     906117
Symptoms: Headache, **Incorrect dose administered,** Pain, **Product preparation issue**
Write-up: the **patient received five times the recommended dosage;** the patient received the unreconstituted dosage; body aches; headaches;

---

**VAERS ID:**     906009
**Incorrect dose administered**
Write-up: **Full vial of 0.3ml concentrated vaccine administered undiluted with normal saline.**

---

**VAERS ID:**     903194
**Product preparation issue**
Write-up: **Patient may have received undiluted Pfizer COVID-19 vaccine 0.3 ml= ~120 mcg**

---

**VAERS ID:**     914325
**Product preparation error**
Write-up: **The patient was accidentally given an "undiluted" dose of COVID vaccine.**

---

---

**VAERS ID:** 908858

**Product preparation error**

**Write-up: On administering Pfizer-BioNTech COVID-19 Vaccine 12/15/20 at 9:15 PM to recipient staff member, vaccinator did not dilute vial and administered undiluted vaccine, resulting in an estimated 5 -fold increase over the intended dose and at an increased concentration.**

---

**VAERS ID:** 903888

**Product dispensing error, Product preparation issue**

Write-up: Pfizer-Biotech covid-19 vaccine eua, **pt denies any sign or symptoms of side effects or adverse events at this time.** Pt was administered dosage the was reconstituted with 0.8ml instead of 1.8ml. Was not until 4th dose for 4th pt was drawn up was it realized there was not enough to complete 6 injections from multi dose vial.

---

**PAITENT GOT MIXED BRAND DOSES AND DIED 5 DAYS LATER**
**VAERS ID: 1038234**

Age: 84.0 Sex: Female Location: Massachusetts Vaccinated: 2021-01-14

Vaccination / Manufacturer          Lot / Dose          Site / Route

COVID19 (COVID19 (PFIZER-BIONTECH))

**Administered by: Senior Living**

Symptoms: Condition aggravated, Death, Dementia, Mental impairment, Pyrexia, Urinary tract infection, **Wrong product administered**

SMQs: Neuroleptic malignant syndrome (broad), Anticholinergic syndrome (broad), Dementia (narrow), Noninfectious encephalitis (broad), Noninfectious encephalopathy/delirium (broad), Noninfectious meningitis (broad), **Medication errors**

(narrow), **Drug reaction with eosinophilia and systemic symptoms** syndrome (broad)

**Write-up: First dose Pfizer given at assisted living on 1/14/21** she was subsequently admitted to hospital and **got her second dose but Moderna was given instead** of Pfizer on 2/8/21. She had been improving but in the days following the Moderna vaccine she developed fever and then her mental status declined. She was discharged back to assisted living. Suspected UTI, and moderate dementia, placed on hospice (2/12/21). **Died on 2/13/21.**

---

A young demon asked the Devil:

"How did you manage to bring
so many souls to hell?"

The Devil answered: "I instilled fear
in them!"

Answers the youngster: "Great job!
And what were they afraid of? Wars?
Hunger?"

Answers the Devil: "No, they were afraid of disease!"

From the young demon: "Does this mean they didn't get sick? Are they not dead?
There was no rescue for them?" The Devil answered: "No . . . they got sick, died,
and the rescue was there." The young demon, surprised, answered: "Then I don't
understand???" The Devil answered: "You know they believed the only thing they
have to keep at any cost is their lives.

They stopped hugging, greeting each other. They've moved away from each other.
They gave up all social contacts and everything that was human! Later they ran out
of money, lost their jobs, but that was their choice because they were afraid for their
lives, that's why they quit their jobs without even having bread.

They believed blindly everything they heard and read in the papers.
They gave up their freedoms, they didn't leave their own homes literally anywhere.
They stopped visiting family and friends. The world turned into such a concentra-
tion camp, without forcing them into captivity.
They accepted everything!!!

Just to live at least one more miserable day . . .

And so living, they died every day!!! And that's how it was very easy for me to take
their miserable souls to hell..... "

                    -Author Unknown

# Endnotes

[i] https://www.nobelprize.org/prizes/medicine/1913/richet/biographical/

[ii] https://www.nobelprize.org/prizes/medicine/1913/richet/speech/

[iii] From Nobel Lectures, Physiology or Medicine 1901-1921, Elsevier Publishing Company, Amsterdam, 1967.

[iv] https://www.jacionline.org/article/S0091-6749(04)01398-3/pdf
Excerpts taken from *Clinical Features and Severity Grading of Anaphylaxis* published by Simon G. A. Brown, MBBS, FACEM, PhDa Hobart, Tasmania, Australia

# Additional Reading

**FDA Portal for VAERS Research Data (Vaccine Adverse Reactions Database)**
https://medalerts.org/vaersdb

**Author's Blog**
www.estateartistry.com/blog

**Uncensored Information Platforms**
www.bitchute.com
www.corbettreport.com

**The Flexner Report - 1910**
https://archive.org/details/carnegieflexnerreport

**How the Flexner Report hijacked natural medicine**
https://www.cancertutor.com/flexner-report/

1e8a1092-d9f1-42ba-90bd-c8022894176eR01